Motorsailers

Also by Dag Pike

Power Boats in Rough Seas
The History of Motor Boats

Motorsailers

Dag Pike

David McKay Company, Inc.
New York

Library of Congress Catalog Card Number: 76–19923
ISBN 0–679–50695–0
Printed in Great Britain

Published in Great Britain by
Stanford Maritime Limited
12 Long Acre, London WC2E 9LP

Contents

Illustrations

Photographs on page 55 courtesy *Yachting Monthly*; page 92, Brian Manby; page 216, Anthony Reynolds; page 220, Barry Picthall.

I wish to express my grateful thanks to the many firms and individuals who have given both their time and assistance to produce material for this book.

1.1 *Blue Leopard*, perhaps the ultimate in motorsailers. Designed by Laurent Giles & Partners and built in wood by Wm Osborne of Littlehampton, she is 111′ 6″ × 75′ × 19′ × 9′ 6″, equipped with two Rolls-Royce C8TFLM diesels, and capable of 15 knots under sail or power. Her very light displacement and fine lines contribute to this excellent performance.

1 Introduction

If you asked most people connected with boats whether a particular boat was a motorsailer or not, they could give a ready answer. However, if you asked the same people to define a motorsailer, they would be much more hesitant. It is very difficult to define any particular type as boats tend to range across a spectrum from racing power craft to racing sailing yachts; there are no clear-cut divisions, rather, a gradual transition of types.

To write on motorsailers first requires an answer to the question of what a motorsailer is. Obviously it must be able to both sail and motor effectively, but then so can many auxiliary yachts that are clearly not motorsailers. The answer, I think, lies in the ability to sail and motor in rough conditions. This rules out the auxiliary sailing yacht where the motor is mainly used for manoeuvring in harbour or in calms. It also rules out motor cruisers with steadying sails, which would be unable to make headway on a desired course in rough seas under sail alone. My definition of a motorsailer is a boat which by using either sails or engine independently is able to make good progress in adverse conditions. This still leaves a certain vagueness — what is good progress and what are adverse weather conditions? One would be safe in saying that good progress means going in the direction in which you want to travel at a reasonable speed; adverse weather could be conditions in which you wish you had stayed in harbour.

The ability to motor or sail at will, or a combination of both, would appear to offer the best of all worlds, and if motorsailers offer so much, why doesn't everyone rush out and buy them? The reason is that any such boat must be a compromise, and it is unlikely to be really efficient in any one aspect. This normally resolves itself around the question of speed, and anyone who wants speed under power buys a planing speed boat, while those who want speed under sail buy a 'pure' sailing boat, perhaps with an auxiliary. There is less compromise in these craft, but also less flexibility. A motorsailer could thus be considered a middle-of-the-road design, trying to give a bit of everything and not really succeeding at any of them. This should not be, as the true motorsailer is a very successful cruising boat, and this is its prime attraction. The compromise between motor and sail varies considerably between various designs, some having more emphasis on sail than on power. The range of choice is large and the prospective purchaser has a wide variety to choose from.

As it is now an increasingly popular type of yacht, several firms are trying to cash in on this market by describing their products as motorsailers when strictly speaking they do not come within the category, for various reasons. Size is an important part of the definition, otherwise there will be difficulty in meeting the requirement to make good progress in adverse conditions. It is difficult to give a definite size below which a boat no longer qualifies as a motorsailer, but I would think that the line should be drawn around the 25 ft mark. This is not to say that those below this size are unsatisfactory, but their use would be restricted to more sheltered waters. Some larger boats should also have the same restriction on use, but this is due to poor design and/or construction.

Two quite distinctive types of craft have evolved to fill the motorsailer role. The motor-oriented boats are characterized by a full, heavy displacement type of hull, often double ended, which should make for sea-kindliness. They have the appearance of being strongly and well constructed, and in most cases they do not belie their appearance. Tan sails are often fitted and this adds to the effect of a sound, no-nonsense sea boat. The sailing-oriented motorsailer has a lighter, finer appearance, yet there is still the

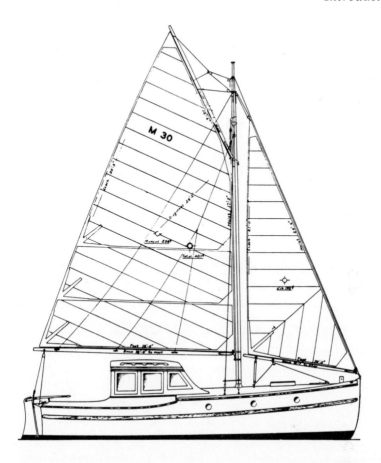

1.2   A motorsailer design by Gordon Munro, from which the first boat was launched in 1936. She was 30′ × 28′ 3″ × 9′ 6″ × 3′ 3″ and powered by a marine conversion of a contemporary Ford V-8 car engine. The deckhouse was completely enclosed and protected the engine hatches, controls and wheel steering position; the self-contained and self-bailing cockpit was intended for use when under sail.

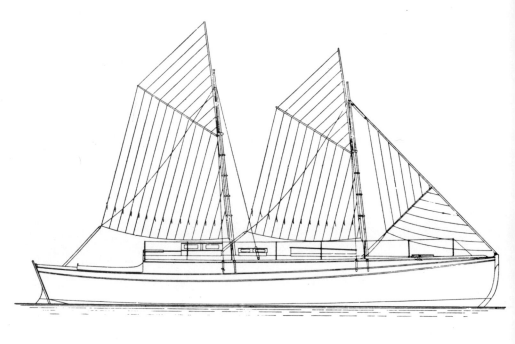

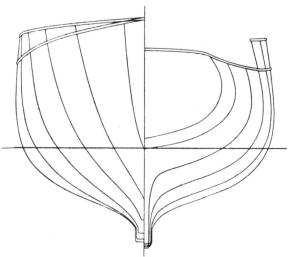

1.3   *Nornodeste*, designed by James A Smith, MINA as a seagoing motor cruiser with auxiliary schooner rig and comfortable accommodation. She measured 41′ 11″ × 9′ × 3′ 5″ and with a 30 h.p. Gardner paraffin engine achieved 9 knots on trials.

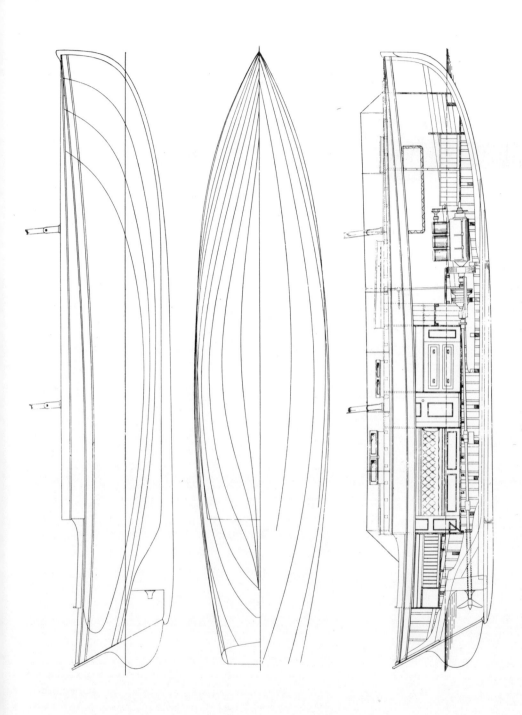

same rugged quality underneath. As the accent is on sailing the hull has finer lines than of the motor types so that it is more easily driven. Some owners and builders prefer the term 'full-powered auxiliaries' to emphasize the sailing qualities – or diminish the power element. Because hulls are not designed primarily for speed, it is possible to place more emphasis on seaworthiness. The difference between motorsailer hulls and those of fast motor and sailing boats demonstrates how much has to be sacrificed in order to obtain maximum speeds.

Again because of the reduced emphasis on speed, motorsailers tend to be very comfortable in terms of motion in a seaway and the size and arrangement of accommodation. This comfort requirement is also seen in a common feature, the wheelhouse or steering shelter. This is a rare structure on a sailing boat proper, where the need to have a clear view of the sails is considered more important than protection for the crew, and where windage is considered detrimental.

The emphasis on comfort combined with a solid, reliable, seaworthy boat is reflected in the type of person who owns a motorsailer. Characteristically he is middle-aged or older, and usually a family man. The motorsailer offers comfortable cruising with the ability to take along family and friends as required, yet it can be handled with a minimum of crew and so also gives the opportunity to escape from family and friends. However, in describing the average owner, it is not my intention to give the impression that he is staid and unadventurous: if this were the case he probably would not have bought a boat in the first place. In fact, the motorsailer is the ideal yacht with which to explore unknown shores. As a cruising boat it approaches the ideal, and its quiet and unobtrusive image combined with less strenuous physical effort in handling are probably the reasons why it appeals to the older person.

The comfort that is expected from a motorsailer is another reason why a boat under 25 ft long does not really come into the category. It would not be suitable for extended passages in any degree of comfort, for in any boat under that size comfort down below becomes fairly minimal; headroom is usually the first thing to suffer. However, motorsailers under this size are produced, and it would be fair to consider them 'inshore' motorsailers.

1.4   At the small end of the range, this Swedish 20-footer is suitable for inshore waters, but not a true motorsailer in terms of ability to make progress in adverse conditions. (Marieholm MS20)

Before the term 'motorsailer' came into common usage, there was a type of boat called the 'fifty-fifty'. The inference was that the boat was half motor and half sail, and in these early days of development the percentage related to the performance under sail compared with that of a pure sailing boat. Other designs were the 'sixty-forty' or 'forty-sixty', denoting emphasis on either power or sailing performance.

The term 'fifty-fifty' has been largely dropped in favour of 'motorsailer', mainly because of the feeling that the fifty-fifty neither motored nor sailed very well. Present-day designs usually show a bias one way or the other, and it would be difficult to select an example which was exactly in the middle (though some sorts neither sail nor motor well). As design progresses sailing performance is generally able to approach that of the pure sailing boat, while the efficiency under power is kept up to displacement motor cruiser levels. In time, only expense will prevent people choosing a motorsailer as a cruising yacht, as to provide both means of propulsion at an efficient level is more expensive than just one.

Historically the motorsailer is not new. When engines were first put into boats, the sails were kept because the engines were unreliable, and because they offered an alternative and free means of propulsion. Many of the first boats to be fitted with engines were only converted sailing craft anyway. As engines became more reliable, so the emphasis on sail was reduced and sailing boats came to be used only for pleasure, though with engines to help in manoeuvring, or provide propulsion in calm or adverse conditions. The type was reborn when engine development reached the stage where small and efficient units could be fitted in sailing hulls to give reasonable performance under both sail and motor. There was still a considerable reduction in both aspects, but as engines and sails have increased in efficiency, the motorsailer has become a more sophisticated proposition. With modern high-speed diesels, efficient hull forms and synthetic fibre sails on modern rigs, it has really come into its own.

The interesting thing about this development is that it has produced characteristic hull shapes. The motor-oriented type has developed from the motor fishing vessel and the similarity of the hull shapes is very pronounced, particularly above the waterline. Below the waterline the motorsailer has a relatively reduced draft to improve its cruising capabilities. The sailing-oriented hull relates more to that of pure sailing boat although it often retains some of the characteristic appearance of the traditional working vessel. Again the draft is generally less than on the pure sailing boat in order to allow greater flexibility in using small harbours, but this can also reduce sailing efficiency, particularly to windward.

It is surprising to find a yacht which occupies a position between power and sailing craft having such a definite character of its own. For a middle-of-the-road type it is surprisingly individual, and this is perhaps its attraction. In many respects it can be seen as a protest, a return to reality and seamanship, which the quest for speed and mass acceptability has tended to brush aside. More and more boating tends to be carried out in sheltered waters and this is reflected in design. For the more adventurous, reliable engines and higher speeds enable a hasty retreat to be made from the open sea. This has contributed to a reduced demand for seaworthiness, and it is good to see this aspect of design being perpetuated.

Motorsailers always seem to attract admiring glances from other boat owners. I am sure that there is a touch of envy, as though they secretly wish that they had a more seamanlike boat and had not been swayed by the glamour of their faster machines. However, the wheel is gradually turning full circle, and attempts are now being made to glamorize the motorsailer, sometimes at the expense of its seamanlike characteristics. Progress in design is important, and is often justified as giving people what they want. It is noticeable how attempts to glamorize a boat of any type often lead to a reduction in its seaworthiness. The present appeal of the motorsailer is in its restrained, dignified, yet eager shape, and its ability to perform well in different roles. This appeal may be lost if the glamour image takes over, but if clever designers are able to get the best of both worlds, progress may be made.

The fact that many of the features of motorsailers are unique means that many of the problems associated with them are also unique, as are their solutions. For too long the motorsailer has been seen as a hybrid type of boat with many bad features resulting from unsatisfactory compromises. That they are now a distinct category in their own right is beyond dispute, and the fact that

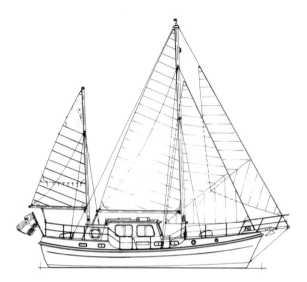

1.5 Three different conceptions of the power-oriented motorsailers sometimes referred to as 'trawler yachts'. The type tends towards heavy displacement, long-keel profiles with little overhang, diesel power and enclosed wheelhouses, all characteristic of working craft from cold northern waters. Steel construction, double-ended full hulls, bulwarks in addition to lifelines, ample tankage and low rigs are also typical. There is commonly some sort of cockpit or open-air steering position additional to that inside the wheelhouse. (Fales Navigator 32/33, Rogger 12-50M, Lunstroo design)

they have many enviable features not found on other types is being realized by an increasing band of discerning owners.

Having established the motorsailer as a unique class of boat, what are its advantages apart from the obvious one of being able to progress efficiently under either sail or motor? It probably represents the ideal cruising boat for those who have to keep to a timetable. This does not mean immunity to bad weather, but rather that the weather has to be fairly bad before one has to consider altering plans. Similarly, one is not forced to run for shelter at the first sign of deteriorating conditions, and this makes the boat suitable for open sea passages lasting several days or longer where more extreme conditions may be met and no shelter is available. Provided the boat is soundly constructed and the superstructure not too vulnerable, bad weather can be faced with reasonable equanimity, although there will be some discomfort.

By having adequate power and rig one is relying wholly on neither. Without wind, good progress can be made under motor, with the sails used for steadying in any swell. If there is too much wind then the boat can heave-to in the safest direction, by motoring slowly to windward. If headwinds are encountered, progress can still be made in the desired direction. Full advantage can be taken of favourable winds, enjoying the peace of sailing, yet knowing the engine is available if a tide has to be caught, or you want to make harbour before the pubs close. The main advantage is that there is a real alternative if either the motor or the sails fail, so that the boat is fairly self-sufficient.

Of course there are disadvantages. Obviously, the purist who hates having a motor in any shape or form will not touch a motorsailer, nor will the person who wants to race, under either sail or power. Their approach must be one of no compromise and these boats are not for them. It is this middle-of-the-road aspect which

1.6 A recently designed steel motorsailer, built in Holland but exemplifying a type seen in American and European waters for some years. This is one of the smaller examples (67′ 4″ × 46′ 4″ × 15′ 9″ × 8′ 4″), but with a displacement of 67 tons. The steel hull is standard, but the interior layout and finish is variable. There is separate crew and guest accommodation, and lavish provision of domestic appliances and their necessary electrical and plumbing systems. (Jongert 19m)

is probably the main disadvantage of the type and the reason why
it is not everyone's cup of tea. Yachtsmen are very prone to take
up definite, uncompromising positions, and be either power or
sail enthusiasts: the motorsailer does not cater to such a stand.
Although early designs were sometimes poor compromises which
probably lead to a poor reputation, production boats now offer a
much better solution, and I can see their popularity increasing
rapidly as good qualities are recognized. The trend is there and a
wide variety of designs are available, offering different approaches
to the concept. It is to be hoped that there will not be too many
cheap imitations that destroy the image of quality and reliability
now being gained. Hopefully, this book, by pointing out the
pitfalls and elaborating the qualities, will help to maintain the
standard of motorsailers.

1.7 A modern production fibreglass motorsailer/full-powered auxiliary
(41′ 3″ × 34′ × 13′ 10″ × 4′ 2″). The hull is long-keeled with high topsides
made apparently lower by the broad dark band, and the rig is either ketch or
sloop and clearly meant for sailing. There is adequate working space on foredeck,
side decks and stern, yet the long coachroof, raised cockpit and ample beam
amidships and aft allow a roomy walk-through interior with after cabin, large
engineroom, and two heads. (Morgan Out Island 41)

2 Hull Design

When a naval architect sets out to design the hull of a boat, he starts off with a blank sheet of paper, but with a mind that is far from blank. The clean paper gives him apparently unlimited scope, but the shape finally produced will result from the experience of the many boats he will have known and designed previously, combined with the years of gradual development of hull shapes for many purposes, throughout the world. When the vast number of different hull shapes already produced are considered, one may well ask how there is scope for fresh design and why the optimum hull shapes for a particular purpose have not been found already.

The answer lies in the fact that the hull of a boat involves a great number of varying and interrelated factors. Most of these can only be optimized at the expense of others, and by sharpening a curve here or fining a line there the designer attempts to improve the compromise for the particular purpose for which the boat is intended. He is not always successful, but the gradual improvement seen in yacht design shows that, on balance, he is gaining ground.

Most boats are designed with a fairly heavy accent in one particular direction – seaworthiness, safety, optimum performance under sail, and so on. It is only when one comes to motorsailer design that there is no emphasis in any particular direction, and yet, whether by accident or design, motorsailers have developed a character of their own, demonstrating how designing for a particular purpose is likely to produce a characteristic type of boat as different people come up with similar solutions.

When it comes to designing any hull, there is no question of producing what looks like a suitable shape and then adding the rig, sails, engine and accommodation, hoping that the finished product will turn into a cohesive whole. All of these elements must be considered when the design of the hull is commenced because each of them will have a bearing on it, as will be shown later. One of the first things which has to be considered is the material from which the hull is to be built, and the designer is likely to have this dictated to him by his client.

All of the materials used for boatbuilding have characteristics which give both advantages and disadvantages. For example, certain shapes cannot be made from certain materials except at great expense, and the designer must be careful to work within the limits of his material. There is a wide choice of materials available – wood, fibreglass, metal, ferrocement – and it is not uncommon to find a combination of these used in one hull.

Wood in one form or another can be adapted to most hull shapes, but complicated shapes become expensive. It is best used on hulls which have gradual, smooth flowing lines that suit the bending characteristics of wood. The traditional methods of building in wood have been supplemented by the use of hot and cold moulded construction which gives greater versatility in shape, as well as light weight with strength. Plywood in sheet form has been used, but its use in hulls is limited as it can only be bent in one plane at a time. The use of timber in motorsailer construction is now generally limited to one-off designs, or to larger craft which are produced on what amounts to a one-off basis.

For production motorsailers, fibreglass is used almost universally. It allows complex shapes to be produced with a very high standard of finish and durability, the only limitation regarding the complexity of the shape being whether it will come out of the mould cleanly and be free of 'hard spots'. The beautiful smooth shapes of many modern motorsailers are achieved by the designer making full use of the material's capabilities.

The necessity for a fairly expensive mould to produce good quality fibreglass hulls means that its use is normally limited to those boats for which a production run of at least ten is being considered. There is another method of fibreglass construction which requires a much simpler mould whereby one-off construction is more practical. This is foam sandwich construction, where the hull or deck shape is constructed over a skeleton mould in easily workable foam plastic sheets, on which fibreglass is then laid up on each side. The main snag is the difficulty in achieving a satisfactory finish on the outside, and of achieving total adhesion between the core and outer skins.

The use of steel or aluminium is usually restricted to larger hulls, partly because of the less intricate shaping required and partly

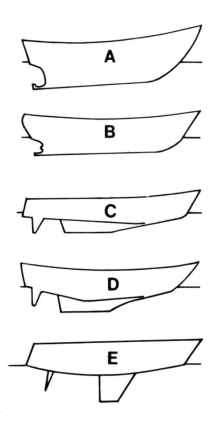

2.1 Hull shapes range from those derived from working boats and power craft (A, B) to a more theoretical approach to motorsailing (C). While (E) is a more or less pure sailing form with a different 'lid' and rig, (D) shows some concessions to powering.

because of the weight factor. There is a minimum thickness of plating which is acceptable, having regard to its stiffness, and this can make a small hull rather on the heavy side if steel is used. Aluminium is better in this respect but it is comparatively expensive, and to form it properly requires specialized equipment and expertise. With metal hulls a lot of effort is required if a satisfactory finish is to be achieved, and the prevention of corrosion can be a major factor. Even where a batch of boats are to be built to a single design, much of the work has to be repeated for each hull.

Ferrocement is gaining ground in yacht construction. At first sight it seems a most unlikely material, but it offers many advantages, not least of which are cost and simplicity of hull construction. It offers the flexibility of shape and ease of repair of fibreglass and yet does not require an expensive mould. However the same standard of surface finish is not achieved with most present methods, except where a female mould is (rarely) used for a production run. For the home builder and for one-off designs, ferrocement is a very realistic proposition, particularly for motorsailers where weight is not as critical as for performance designs.

The introduction of fibreglass and the greater freedom of design which it gave was largely responsible for the dramatic improvement in boat design over the last few years. Certainly the smaller motorsailers have only become common since its use, and few hulls under 40 ft are built of anything else these days. In the larger sizes, mainly because they are more likely to be custom built, the choice is more varied, but as production hulls get larger and larger the use of fibreglass becomes more prevalent. Development has now made this a very reliable material, although there have been many early examples of construction which tended to give it a bad name.

The prime requirement of any hull which is to operate in a seaway is that it shall be seaworthy. This is a somewhat vague and ill-defined term, and seaworthiness tends to be judged in relation to other boats rather than absolutely. There is no way in which it can be measured, except perhaps in terms of the type of seas which a vessel can be expected to cope with. Three main factors affect seaworthiness: length, shape and strength. The first of these is frequently specified in the designer's brief so that he

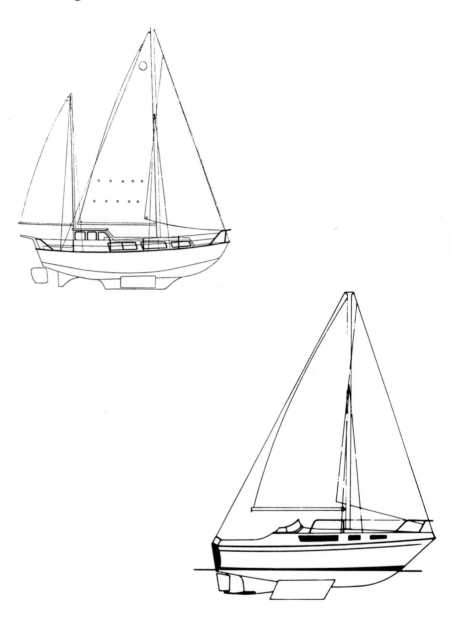

2.2 A steel and a fibreglass hull where the convenience of a long main keel, protective skeg and bilge keels have resulted, probably inevitably, in large areas of wetted surface which will increase drag, particularly at lower speeds. (Roamer 36, Halmatic 8.80)

is left with the shape of the hull and its strength to ensure that it is adequate for its intended purpose.

A motorsailer is primarily a cruising boat and will be expected to be capable of making extended passages in open water provided that she is of a reasonable size, say over 30 ft. Smaller boats will usually be restricted more to coastal operation where it is possible to seek shelter should conditions deteriorate. The larger motor-sailers should be reasonably designed and equipped to survive severe weather. Absolute safety can never be guaranteed at sea, but there should be reasonable anticipation of conditions. While winds over force 8 are comparatively rare, they do occur on at least a few occasions each year in most sea areas. If a motorsailer is designed to survive in force 8 winds and seas then it will probably have a sufficient reserve of strength to cope with even worse conditions. In these extreme conditions the stresses to which a hull is subjected depend a great deal on how the craft is handled. Shape is not especially critical; a hull designed to operate in force 8 seas will be equally at home in even worse conditions provided it has good reserve of strength.

One of the difficulties in design is first to know what the stresses on a hull are likely to be, and second, to evaluate the strength of a proposed design. Classification societies such as Lloyds issue tables of scantlings for various sizes of yachts and any reputable designer and builder will meet or exceed these. This is fine when working with wood or steel, but with fibreglass the strength of the material and the completed hull shell depends a great deal on how it was laid up rather than on the material that went into it. There is no really satisfactory way of testing completed hulls.

Most firms building motorsailers exercise strict quality control of fabrication. To compensate for any inadequacies in the lay-up, and because of the difficulty in knowing what stresses a boat will be subjected to, the hull is usually considerably over-designed to give a good margin of safety. It is rare to hear of a hull itself failing these days, the superstructure being much more vulnerable. The answer for the intending purchaser is to rely on either the reputation of the yard building the boat or the watchful eye of one of the classification societies. The main requirements here are seaworthiness, speed, comfort and stability. The order of priority will depend on the type of boat required, and is likely to be specified rather generally by the client. The designer's job is to combine all of these features, putting emphasis where he considers it important and producing a workable compromise at the end.

We have already seen how seaworthiness relates to shape, length and strength. It is the first of these, shape, which is most considered. Many of the terms used have to be relative rather than absolute because in discussing hulls it is the relationship of one part to another, not the absolute measurements, which matters.

When the sea is from ahead or astern it is the form of the bow and stern which will have a large effect on the behaviour of the boat. Whatever shape is chosen, it is important that the two ends balance. If the bow is full, the stern should also be full otherwise the finer end of the boat will submerge too readily when the fuller end rises to a wave. Fullness here means plenty of volume, giving plenty of buoyancy. If the bow were fine and the stern full, the bow would not lift readily and the boat would be very wet in a head sea, tending to go through the waves rather than over them. In a following sea, the bow should again at least match the stern, otherwise when the stern lifts to an overtaking wave, the too-fine bow will submerge, producing a fulcrum about which the boat can pivot under the force of the overtaking wave and take up the classic broaching position. There should be plenty of buoyancy at both ends so that she will lift readily to waves; also plenty of freeboard so that the bow (or stern) has to be submerged a long way before the wave crest finally breaks on board. Additional freeboard is often created a little artificially by having bulwarks, which can have a beneficial effect without destroying the pleasing appearance of a hull.

The actual shape of the bow in transverse section is not too critical in relation to head or stern seas, providing the volume is adequate. Some designers utilize a concave shape or flare. Water from an attacking wave is deflected away from the boat, thus hopefully making it drier. To achieve a flared shape the lower part of a bow section has to be narrow and the buoyancy tends to be concentrated towards the top: this will exaggerate pitching. A convex cross-section will provide more initial buoyancy but will not deflect the water away so readily, and some designs end up with a combination of convex shape for the lower part and concave for the upper, in an attempt to keep the best of both. A

2.3 Well-matched
bow and stern shapes
on a hull derived from
Scandinavian motor
fishing boats.
(Finnsailer 35)

small knuckle in the bow sections may be introduced to 'peel' the water away.

There is a lot more choice in the shape of a stern as it does not have to be forced through the water. However, in a rough following sea the waves will be overtaking the boat, and it is desirable that the stern offers as little resistance as possible to them. A pointed stern will achieve this, and the classic double-ended shape is one of the best from the seaworthiness point of view. The number of motorsailers utilizing this shape shows the emphasis which is placed on seaworthiness in this class. An acceptable compromise which was introduced to meet yacht racing rules, but which also provides more space in the after end, is the truncated counter stern. Here the fine shape underwater at the stern opens out into a short counter which terminates in a transom; it remains above water in normal conditions.

Operating stern to the seas opens up the possibility of being swept to one side or the other in a potential broach. Offering the least resistance to an oncoming wave helps, but if the wave is breaking, even small resistance will be magnified as the surface water will be in motion. The effect of the fast-moving surface water on the upper part of the hull will be resisted by the lower part, which if the boat has sufficient draft will still be in relatively stable water. It is difficult to define sufficient draft as a lot will depend on the size of the breaking wave and the position of the boat in it. At the point of breaking the forward moving water is probably quite deep, but immediately afterwards is unlikely to be more than two or three feet deep. In really heavy seas this figure will be exceeded, but perhaps one should not be running before the seas under these conditions.

Adequate draft for rough conditions is likely to be somewhere around twice the depth of the moving water, but in fact draft is much more likely to be dictated by considerations of operating from tidal harbours and adequate windward sailing performance. Motorsailers seem to average about 1 ft of draft for every 10 ft of hull length, between 35 ft and 60 ft.

When a boat is operating in a beam sea, it is its beam in relation to length and the shape of the transverse section amidships which will affect the stability and behaviour. The general ratio of length to beam is 3 : 1 and most motorsailers come fairly close to this ratio.

Where attempts have been made to get higher speeds the ratio may increase to 3.5:1. The shape of the transverse sections is usually moderate on motorsailers as this tends to make for a form which is comfortable at sea. If the section has a hard turn at the bilge it will be more stable, but the motion will be more violent. Conversely, if the bilge is slack, i.e. the side of the boat runs down to the keel without any sharp angle or curve, there will be a loss of stability which will have to be compensated for with ballast, which also affects its behaviour.

Obviously stability is important at all times, but it is in a beam sea where the surface of the water may be inclined as much as 18° from the horizontal that it can be critical. When a breaking wave is striking the hull beam-on, greater capsizing forces are exerted. Stability is part of the overall seaworthiness of a hull, but unlike seaworthiness in general, it is possible to calculate with some degree of accuracy how stable a hull is. (What is not so easy to estimate are the varied forces which act to capsize a boat.) Stability is the ability of a hull to return to the upright when inclined by an external force. It is most critical in the transverse plane, but it can be calculated equally well in the fore and aft plane.

At rest in still water the hull of a boat has two forces which act on it: gravity acting vertically downwards through the centre of gravity (CG), and buoyancy acting vertically upwards through the centre of buoyancy (CB). Both of these forces are individually equal to the weight of the boat, and in still water they are equal and opposite so that it is in equilibrium. The centre of gravity of a boat (or any other mass) remains in a fixed position unless weights are moved about in the hull, or taken off or added. The compensating movement of the centre of gravity will be towards a weight which is added or away from one removed, and the amount of this movement will be in relation to the weight moved and its distance from the centre of gravity. At sea the only significant and likely alteration to weight distribution will be the movements of the crew about the boat and the using up of fuel. Both of these will have a small effect, although the gradual using up of fuel may have a longer term effect, particularly as it is often stored in the bottom of the boat, and as some motorsailers have large tanks.

The centre of buoyancy is the centre of gravity of the volume of

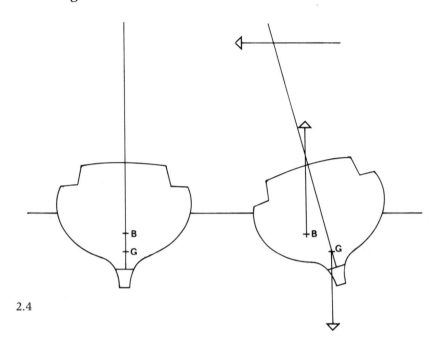

2.4

water which is displaced by the hull. As water is a homogeneous fluid, this means that the centre of buoyancy is at the geometric centre of the underwater part of the hull. When a boat heels, the underwater shape changes and the centre of buoyancy moves accordingly. The two forces work opposite to each other, as the centre of buoyancy has been displaced towards the more deeply immersed side of the hull. In this position the upward force of buoyancy acting through the CB serves to tend to right the boat in conjunction with the downward force of gravity, until the two centres are once more in a line vertically one above the other (2.4).

As a boat heels further over, with most designs of hull, the centre of buoyancy will move less quickly, the amount it moves being determined by the change in shape of the immersed hull. The centre of gravity will remain on the centreline of the boat, but as it heels, the upper part of the centreline plane will move towards the heeled side and the lower part away, so that the height of the centre of gravity has to be considered when establishing the stability of a hull. If the centre of gravity is fairly high in the hull, the range of stability will be lower, as a time will come as the boat heels when the centre of gravity is directly above the centre of buoyancy and the righting moment disappears. Any further heeling is liable to end in a capsize.

This sort of situation can be found in motor boats where no ballast is carried and the centre of gravity is relatively high. The increased beam found on most motor boats means that there is usually stability up to 40–50° of heel, which is adequate for most practical purposes. In a sailing boat, however, the heeling effect of the wind on the sails has to be allowed for; also the considerable weight of the mast and sails will raise the centre of gravity. The shape of the hull alone cannot provide sufficient stability to compensate, and ballast has to be added low down to lower the centre of gravity so that it remains below the centre of buoyancy.

It would be easy to add enough ballast so that there would be no doubts about the stability, but excessive ballast has the effect of making a boat very stiff. This means that the righting moment on the hull is excessive and it will come back upright very quickly, making life on board very uncomfortable and adding to the stresses on the rig. Excessive ballast naturally also adds to the weight of the boat and will reduce performance, so its amount and position have to be calculated carefully.

To gain maximum effect with a minimum of weight, the ballast should be placed as low as possible. On some yachts the ballast is placed at the end of a fin keel, but this is extreme, and it is more usually placed along the vertical length of a fin or the bottom of a long keel, the depth of keel being usually determined by hull shape and practical draft considerations rather than solely for maximum performance, and occasionally by cost.

How does stability affect motorsailers? Obviously, they must have sufficient stability to compensate for the heeling effect of the wind on the sails and rig, but as motorsailers do not generally carry a lot of canvas or very tall rigs large amounts of ballast are not necessary. However, as their draft is usually limited to around 10 per cent of the length, which is practical for cruising, the ballast cannot be placed very far below the centre of gravity. This means that its weight has to be increased, as the effect of any ballast is a combination of its weight and its distance from the centre of gravity.

The weight of ballast carried by a yacht is related to the total displacement of the hull, as a ratio. The ballast on a motorsailer is unlikely to exceed one-third of the total displacement except where there is a very definite accent on sailing performance. The ballast has also to be related to other large weights such as the engine and tankage; e.g., in a craft with a heavy engine the ballast ratio will be lower. The ballast ratio will also relate to the sail area and height; with a large sail area additional ballast will be required to maintain the desired stability.

Performance in terms of out-and-out speed is not regarded as a critical aspect of motorsailers, but they must be able to sail and motor efficiently if they are to fulfil their function. The lines do not have to be fined down to the extent found on many sailing boats, and by making a hull with a generous beam and a fairly sharp turn at the bilges, the stability that comes from the shape of the hull is increased. It cannot be increased to that of the hull of a beamy motor boat, but the righting moment derived from the combination of hull shape and ballast can make the motion comfortable.

As the motorsailer is designed primarily as a cruising boat, it should be as versatile as possible to cope with the varying conditions which can be found. A major factor which can limit cruising prospects is deep draft, as it often means having to anchor off instead of finding a comfortable berth in harbour or up a river. In many harbours boats have to dry out and take the bottom, and cruising range may be restricted if these cannot be used. The shape of the keel will have a bearing on this as the boat should take the bottom without placing undue strain on the hull and without assuming undignified angles of trim. The latter demands a fairly level, straight keel, usual only on motor-oriented motorsailers with working boat antecedents. The material also matters: lead or iron are far tougher than fibreglass when supporting the weight of a boat against a hard bottom. The rudder has to be protected against taking any weight, by the keel or a strong skeg deeper than the rudder shaft.

Other factors influence the shape and size of the keel. When a boat is under sail with the wind on the beam or closehauled, the wind, acting through the centre of effort (CE) on the sails, tends to blow it bodily sideways as well as giving forward motion. Leeway is undesirable and is resisted by the hull's being reluctant to move sideways. A deep draft hull will show more reluctance than a shallow one, but will also offer more resistance to forward motion. The designed draft of any motorsailer is a compromise of many factors, but the average found of 10 per cent of the length seems to strike a fairly happy medium. Sailing-oriented designs will usually have a higher ratio in an attempt to reduce leeway and improve performance.

When a boat heels to the wind its draft is slightly reduced and certainly the effective shape of the hull will increase its leeway. One method of improving this situation which designers seem reluctant to use is to fit a centreboard below the keel. Centreboards have suffered in the past from poor design and construction, but modern materials and due regard for the stresses involved should overcome this, and they have started to reappear on some larger racing boats. Protecting the rudder, however, may be more difficult in the absence of a deep keel.

The pressure on the centre of effort of the sails is countered by that on the centre of lateral resistance (CLR) of the hull. It stands to reason that these two must be in a vertical line one above the other if the steering is not to be affected too much. The centre of lateral resistance is the geometric centre of the underwater profile and obviously has to be considered when designing the hull. It will be discussed in much more detail later.

With regard to the sailing aspects of a motorsailer, it is essential that the hull should offer minimum resistance to passing through the water if the sails are to gain maximum effect. Though the sail area on a motorsailer is usually smaller than on a pure sailing boat, it is expected to have reasonable performance under sail. Two main factors affect the speed of a hull through the water at displacement speeds: friction and wave-making resistance. Any hull moving through the water sets up a pattern of waves. Their formation requires energy which is imparted from the hull, thus affecting its rate of progress. At slow speeds the energy drain from the waves is small, friction being much more important, but as speed increases the energy used in wave-making rises rapidly until a point is reached where the boat will not travel faster no matter how much power is applied. This maximum or 'hull' speed is largely a function of the immersed length of the boat: the longer the waterline length the faster it is able to travel in the displacement mode. There is a direct relationship between a displacement boat's speed and the length of wave it makes. At a given speed any boat of any length will make the same length of wave. Designers talk about a speed : length ratio, which in fact is the square root of the waterline length in feet divided into the maximum speed. For most motorsailers this factor will be around 1.3 which for a 36 ft LWL craft gives a top speed of 8 knots if the formula is worked backwards.

Maximum hull speed of a motorsailer will only be reached in strong winds with an efficient rig, but even at lower speeds any saving in wave drag will mean better progress. A hull with fine lines will disperse less energy in forming waves and will thus be more easily driven under sail. However, fining down the lines of a hull will have adverse effects in other directions and a balance must be struck. In most motorsailer designs other considerations outweigh pure sailing performance.

Friction between the hull of the boat and the water also increases with speed, but at higher speeds does not have such a great effect as the wave-making resistance. The resistance due to friction of a smooth hull is related to the area of wetted surface, so if a boat is to be easily driven the underwater surface area should be kept to a minimum. Fine lines will help to achieve this, but attention must be paid to all appendages such as bilge keels, struts, propellers, etc (2.2, 6.3).

While sailing demands an easily driven hull to make the best use of the limited power available, motoring is not so demanding. Most modern motorsailers have sufficient power to push along at somewhere near maximum speed. To utilize engine power efficiently, the designer is more concerned with obtaining a good flow of water around the propeller. This can be done by fining the lines of the lower part of the hull to prevent eddies forming. Under power alone there will be adequate stability from the ballast, but unless some additional stability is achieved from the full hull sections and a hard turn of bilge amidships, the motion is likely to be uncomfortable once the steadying influence of the sails is removed. Surface friction and wave-making resistance are equally important under power.

It might be assumed that in producing a seaworthy hull the designer had done his job, but the comfort aspect is very important if life aboard is going to be all that it should be on a cruising boat, and if the boat is to be fully used and enjoyed. Hardened sailors sometimes scoff at the idea of introducing comfort on board a boat, but here I am referring to the motion and the available space on board, not thick pile carpets. A boat with an easy motion reduces the stresses on the hull, gear and crew so it is something worth seeking. Like seaworthiness, comfort is difficult to define and measure, certainly in absolute terms. One tends to compare the present boat with past boats in the same way that the designer uses past experience in the present design. Comfort and seaworthiness are interrelated to a degree, but the factors which make for a seaworthy boat do not necessarily make for a comfortable one.

We have seen how a full bow and stern make for a seaworthy hull, allowing it to lift over waves rather than go through them. This is fine, but the boat will then try to follow faithfully the contours of every wave, and the resulting motion will be very uncomfortable; it should partially cut through the waves, and the gently flared bow can provide a good compromise. Whatever shape and contours are finally decided on, the result should have smooth cohesive lines without any sudden changes. Sudden changes invariably mean that the water has to make some unnatural alteration in flow in trying to conform to the hull, and this will produce slamming, jolting or some other unpleasant reaction. From the strength point of view, any sudden change in section will introduce stress concentrations.

The shape of the bow and stern largely affect pitching, but it is the transverse shape which has a bearing on the rolling motion. Rolling can be extremely tiring in view of the large changes of angle which are involved, and one of the objects of any boat design must be to reduce it to a reasonable level and make any rolling which does take place of a gentle nature. Violent rolling can make life on board very difficult, apart from the very real danger of personal injury. There are two approaches to reducing rolling, one being the design of the hull and the other damping out the rolling by external means.

Every hull has a characteristic roll period, rather like a pendulum: if it were set rolling artificially it would take a set time to roll each way. At sea problems start when this natural roll period coincides with the period of the waves, as the resulting exaggerated motion becomes very unpleasant and can be dangerous. If all waves were of the same period it would be easy to design a hull with a different roll period, but waves come in all lengths and sizes. What the designer tries to do is make the roll period fairly long, so that at least if it does coincide with that of the waves the motion will not be too violent.

The shape of the hull initially determines the roll period, but it cannot be divorced from the distribution of weight in the hull. A hull which is hemispherical in transverse section will roll gently while a narrow hull with fine lines will roll quickly. In any sailing boat with a ballast keel the weight is concentrated low down and this will speed up the rolling period, but the shape of the keel on which the ballast is mounted will tend to damp rolling.

Damping by external means can be most effective, and is done by introducing surfaces (fins or sails) at right angles to the motion which interact with the water or the air and resist the rolling motion of the boat in the transverse plane. The fluid has to flow from one side of the surface to the other before the boat can roll, and we have already mentioned that the keel can be beneficial in this respect. The motorsailer is fortunate in also having sails which have an excellent damping effect, although without the sails up and running under engine alone, it is at a disadvantage because it still has the heavy ballast keel which shortens the rolling period. If this weight were to be spread out over the bottom of the hull instead of being concentrated, the period would be longer, and in some designs some of the ballast is placed in the bilges. Any weight which can be spread out around the hull such as fuel and water will make the motion more comfortable.

Boats often roll quite heavily in a following sea and here the sails are of little use in damping out the motion as they are not set fore and aft, except in the case of steadying sails on some motor cruisers. The keel will still exercise its damping effect, and bilge keels are sometimes fitted to supplement this; they reduce rolling when under power alone, and also can enable a hull to sit on the bottom in a more upright position. It is refreshing to find something in boat design which can do two jobs, but of course bilge keels increase the wetted area and thus create considerable drag when sailing.

When discussing comfort in relation to hull design, the space available for accommodation has to be considered. The designer's brief will usually indicate the number of berths and the standard of comfort which is sought. While great ingenuity is often shown in making maximum use of available space, the more open space available the better, and the tendency will be to make the shape of the hull as full as possible without detriment to other factors. The sheerline of the deck will often be raised to make adequate headroom below, and high topsides are a notable feature of some very roomy current boats (Chapters 3 and 7).

The last point brings in the question of appearance. Everyone wants their boat to look 'right', but what is 'right' is hard to define. People will tell you when they see it, but the designer has to anticipate this reaction. The accepted traditional shapes really present no difficulties, but attempting innovation can raise objections from the client. The yachtsman is basically conservative, which is reasonable in the absence of any objective yardstick by which to measure performance and appearance.

From all the foregoing you may wonder how any yacht ever gets designed. However, in most cases the resulting craft is reasonably successful. The compromises to be made in designing a motorsailer are more than with other types and this possibly accounts for their long time in developing as a distinct class of boat. Most rate seaworthiness fairly high on their list of priorities. The generous lines are evidence of this, but by delicate fining forward and aft performance under sail is maintained. Moderate draft must reduce seaworthiness to a certain extent, and again sailing performance. This is perhaps not too important in a motorsailer if one is prepared to accept that the engine is always available to make up lost ground if required, but it should not become an excuse for poor sailing qualities.

Within the average motorsailer compromise, only two things really suffer to any great extent. Compared to a pure sailing boat the sailing ability is rather poor, particularly to windward. Accommodation is more restricted than in a pure motor boat, although often more comfortable. The present tendency in motor boat design is to build upwards to get more accommodation on a given waterline length, and a similar trend is noticeable in some motorsailers. Obviously the sails and rig will set an upper limit, but this practice detracts from seaworthiness.

Most motorsailer hulls produced nowadays are the designer's or builder's ideas of what the public wants. With quantity production a fairly moderate approach has to be adopted in order to meet the requirements of as many people as possible. Fortunately there is now a wide variety of production boats on the market, which increases the chances for the individual to choose one which meets his idea of the motorsailer concept. There is little one can do in the way of modification to a standard production boat without great expense and the prospective buyer is cautioned to think at length and in detail about what he wants. The alternative to a production hull is having a boat custom built. Within the range of the production motorsailers, which is up to about 45 ft, there is little to be gained from this approach in terms of cost or other benefits. The end result is unlikely to be much better and the costs will be much higher. If one's requirements are for something larger or markedly different from production craft, a one-off design becomes a possibility if not a must. The compromises are much the same in the larger sizes, but there is much more scope for accommodating them, and of course one is in a better position to get the preferred solution.

Many of the cruising sailing yachts over 50 ft long which are now being built come within the motorsailer category. On these larger craft the draft is often increased above 10 per cent of the length and this improves their sailing qualities. The length:beam ratio is reduced to give a finer shape which can be accepted on larger hulls without sacrificing stability or comfortable accommodation. More efficient rigs and bigger sailplans become necessary, but are also more commonly found. The designer's task becomes easier as the hull gets larger, as many factors are less critical or less difficult to accommodate.

2.5 The relationship between the immersed and above-water hull volumes here is a departure from traditional design. On a medium-sized boat (38′ 8″ × 27′ 6″ × 10′ 1″ × 3′ 9″ or 5′ 6″), high topsides and flush decks give maximum interior space with full walk-through headroom. Horizontal colour banding reduces the apparent height of the hull. The raised open cockpit is virtually set on the deck, as its sole is only just below the amidships deck level. The accommodation is completely contained within the hull, in contrast to the high coachroofs/cabin tops seen on some of the boats in Chapters 3 and 7, where

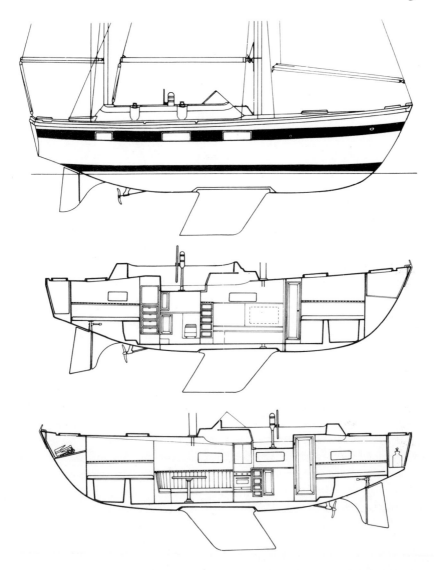

living spaces are particularly enclosed by superstructure. While the implications of a large open cockpit for heavy weather sailing are not ideal, the vulnerable element of large windows and superstructure has been avoided. Other modern tendencies are the deliberate reduction of wetted surface; a wide transom and aft sections, which allow a decent-sized after cabin; optional ketch or sloop rig; and the positioning of the small service areas (galley and head) on either side of the engine compartment where their occasional use means least annoyance from noise and vibration. (Coronado 35)

3 Deck and Superstructure

Among their many functions, the deck and superstructure must be thought of as providing space for working the sails, a top for the accommodation which determines the headroom below, the position from which the boat is controlled, and also as having a big impact on appearance. The interaction of these functions can be seen in the illustrations below, in Chapter 7, and in the examples in the final section. Many of the requirements of the deck and superstructure will conflict, particularly in view of the limited space available; and probably one of the more difficult areas of decision will be the question of how much appearance will be allowed to outweigh practical considerations of handling. From a commercial point of view, looks are important as many boats are purchased by owners who work on the maxim that 'if it looks right it is right' and find appearance a part of their satisfaction in ownership.

One of the major elements is the sheer or deck line. A really straight sheerline is almost unheard of and would look ungainly on a motorsailer. The most common and the traditional line is concave, rising at bow and stern and dipping amidships. It is used a great deal on motorsailers in a fairly pronounced form as it reinforces the traditional appearance, but it does reduce the available headroom amidships where it is most in demand.

Headroom can be increased by the use of a coachroof but this reduces the strength of the deck, and a new trend slowly emerging in motorsailers is the use of reverse sheer in which the deck line rises slightly from the bow and the fore-and-aft deck contour is a convex curve. If this line were carried right aft the appearance would be somewhat bulbous, and it is not unusual for the sheerline to be broken amidships and to drop away into a normal sheer near the stern. A reverse sheer certainly gives plenty of headroom and the convex shape will shed water easily and rapidly. The deck is stronger as it is not broken over the width of the boat and the convex curvature adds to its strength. For most practical considerations it offers advantages and it is mainly on the grounds of appearance that it gained ready acceptance. It is used more on smaller motorsailers where the increased space and headroom is at more of a premium; on large boats there is enough headroom when a flush deck is used, and the traditional concave sheerline gives, even with a coachroof, a shape better suited to the larger boat. Flush decks combined with high topsides are seen in (2.5, 3.2, 7.3).

In conjunction with the sheerline the designer has to determine the position and form of the wheelhouse or shelter, more or less a standard feature. It can dominate the appearance, particularly on motor-oriented motorsailers. This type favours the totally enclosed wheelhouse whereas the sailing-oriented motorsailer tends to have a wheelhouse with an open back which is more correctly termed a shelter. Shelters can be either rigid or collapsible (3.1).

A wheelhouse has to be carefully located if it is to be in harmony with the rest of the boat. To balance the bulk of the wheelhouse, the deck sheer is often exaggerated, the high bow offsetting the superstructure. The wheelhouse is invariably placed over the engine compartment, the raised top allowing full headroom in spite of the raised deck level over the engine. As the position of the engine is variable within limits, it is assumed that the wheelhouse is located on aesthetic grounds, and the engine position to match.

If the floor of the wheelhouse (or cockpit) were at the normal deck level there would be more freedom in its positioning as it would not have to relate to the space below decks except for access. The wheelhouse would stand high above the deck and could only be brought into proportion by fitting high bulwarks. A high wheelhouse means that the boom of the mainsail has to be raised to ensure clearance, and generally the problems of placing the wheelhouse at deck level outweigh any advantages which might be gained. Raised open cockpits are a more recent solution, and on boats with high freeboard there can be full headroom underneath (1.5, 2.5, 3.2, 3.3, 7.1–3).

A steering shelter is a much lighter structure in both appearance and construction. Whereas a wheelhouse becomes an integral part of the boat, the shelter, unless carefully designed, so often looks like an afterthought. It is almost as though the structure and a larger engine have been fitted to a conventional sailing auxiliary in an effort to convert it into a motorsailer. As with the other options, the size and depth of the sheltered area influences layout below decks, and two examples are shown in (3.1).

The practicality of a steering shelter is open to question. The object must be to offer protection from the elements, and certainly it will shelter the occupants from rain. Spray is a different matter: it is associated with wind, and any wind will cause eddies around the back of the shelter which will tend to suck spray in. A little spray entering in this manner can often be more irritating than the large quantities often endured in an open cockpit – at least one then dresses for the job. The after end of the shelter is usually extended aft beyond the side supports and any water running off the top drops straight down into the cockpit, much to the annoyance of any occupants.

Collapsible shelters which hopefully combine the advantages of an open and a sheltered steering position can be even more irritating when it comes to drips and drafts unless they are very carefully constructed. This question of shelter for the steering position is very vexed: what looks very nice and attractive in brochures, can be worse than useless at sea. If good weather protection is required then the only answer is a fully enclosed wheelhouse. A shelter will only stop the worst of the wind and water which are flying about.

Unless the boat has a reverse sheer, it is usual for the forward end of the wheelhouse to slope into the coachroof top which then extends forward to give headroom in the accommodation. A coachroof can help to reduce the effective height of the wheelhouse and improve the appearance. Although a long coachroof can reduce the strength of the deck in a wooden boat, in good fibreglass construction, where the deck, coachroof and wheelhouse are often moulded as one unit, there is little loss in strength. The design 'image' is noticeably influenced by superstructure lines, and it is worth comparing the different boats shown in the text (1.5, 3.3, 3.4, 7.4 *et al*).

At an early stage in design (or in the prospective owner's thinking) a decision has to be made about the crew for which accommodation will be provided. This can affect the deck layout, as it may mean the provision of an after cabin. On larger motorsailers this is a common arrangement to give added privacy, and on smaller ones it is sometimes offered as an alternative to an after cockpit. It can only be achieved on smaller boats at the expense of the after cockpit, and sometimes a reduction in the size of the wheelhouse. This is a slightly self-defeating exercise, as it increases the number of crew who can sleep on board, but reduces the space available on deck, where most time is spent when at sea. Except in large boats, an after cabin usually necessitates an after coachroof or raised deck to give headroom (3.1, 3.2, 3.3). It is more frequently seen in conjunction with a centre cockpit and a shelter over the steering position. Access is then on the forward side of the cabin, and anyone coming out is nicely placed to receive the water pouring off the shelter top. Having an after cabin on a small motorsailer is rather like trying to squeeze a quart into a pint pot, and while it can look very nice and practical at a boat show or tied up alongside, it is an arrangement which wants trying out at sea, before you commit yourself.

Without an after cabin the wheelhouse can open into a good-sized cockpit with the cockpit sole at the same level as that of the wheelhouse. Cockpit lockers can give plenty of stowage for ropes, fenders and all the other bits and pieces of deck gear which one collects and which all seem indispensable. On some designs it is possible to open up the after end of the wheelhouse so that it can combine with the cockpit to make a large airy space in fine weather.

In the search for extra accommodation space there is a tendency to restrict the working area on deck. This really is a false economy, as much of the pleasure of a motorsailer comes from having space

Deck and Superstructure

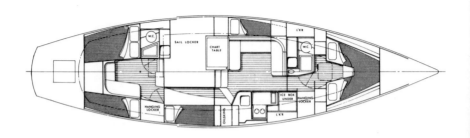

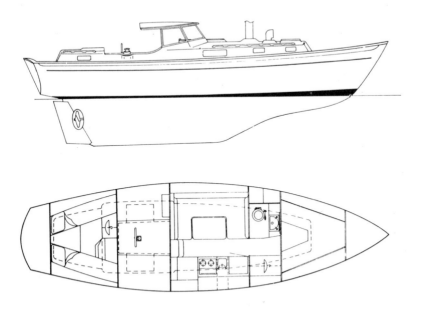

3.1 Short, fairly deep cockpits with steering shelters or semi-wheelhouses, and otherwise conventional coachroof and hull proportions typical of auxiliary cruisers. Both boats have removable fibreglass 'hard-tops' which can be replaced by folding canvas canopies, and canvas side and all-round screens with flexible plastic windows. The centre cockpits are over the engine compartments and provide access to the after cabins. The 35-footer (above) does not have a free-board or cockpit height great enough to allow walk-through access under the cockpit from the saloon, and the available space has been more realistically utilized by deep cockpit lockers for sails and gear. The 48-footer has a fixed for-ward roof section and acrylic windows, and the instruments and steering position are under this fixed structure. The larger overall dimensions permit a walkway between the main saloon and after cabin, though footroom is limited by the curvature of the hull; the after cabin's sole is raised to make a flat surface over the rising stern sections, which are finer than on many recent motorsailers. There is a deep cockpit locker on one side of the engine compartment, and a berth beside the walkway on the other. (Nicholson 48, Rasmus 35)

to move about easily, and these boats are large enough that this can be expected. Safety also comes into it, for if one has to go on deck in bad weather the ability to move on deck quickly and easily can be very important. A wheelhouse can often restrict easy movement as it may be extended as far out to the sides of the boat as possible, and if it has vertical sides, it means leaning out to get past. Good handholds in the right place are partly the answer, but it helps a lot if the sides of the wheelhouse are sloped inward, and side decks are wide enough to move readily on.

On larger motorsailers conflicting demands on deck space are largely overcome by simply having plenty of space everywhere. As no coachroof is required to give headroom below, there are large uncluttered deck areas. Simply because they are uncluttered, moving about the boat in a seaway can be difficult unless lifelines are fitted. On the smaller boat with a coachroof, handholds are fitted along it which makes movement relatively easy and safe.

You may well argue that the guardrails or lifelines are fitted for this purpose, but in my experience these are difficult to hold on to because of their small section, and difficult to brace against because they flex. It is extremely difficult to make guardrails strong and rigid enough so that you can hang onto them. They should be looked on more as a last resort to prevent rolling overboard than as a first line of defence. To be really effective, guardrails would have to be at waist height, but then they would spoil the appearance of the boat. Such rails would also require stanchions braced down to the deck which would obstruct movement.

Most lifelines have the top wire about 2 ft above the deck, with a second wire between this and the deck. The wires are supported by stanchions at regular intervals and there are different ideas about how these stanchions should be fastened to the deck. Stanchions are fitted close to the side of the boat, and are vulnerable when going alongside if there is any overhang or swell. If stanchions are mounted rigidly to the deck and get a knock, they are liable to tear up part of the deck. Many designs aim at producing a point at the base of the stanchion where it will bend or break rather than damage the deck, the argument being that it is easier to fit a new one than to repair the deck. The problem is to make this type sufficiently rigid so that the wire can be tight.

Lifelines invariably terminate at rigid pulpits forward and aft which provide a solid anchor point for the wires, and at the same time a firm support for crew working in these areas. Similar sections of rigid tubing are sometimes fitted alongside the wheelhouse, which makes it easier to negotiate this obstruction and provides better support for the stanchions. Another place where a rigid tubular guard is sometimes fitted is on each side of the mast to give support when working at the halliard winches or reefing. Whatever type and wherever rails or lifelines are fitted, they should be strong and not have any slack. To grab a slack lifeline can upset balance quicker than anything else, and the additional momentum makes the chance of something bending or breaking that much greater.

One way of improving the practicality of guardrails or lifelines is to combine them with bulwarks. They increase reserve buoyancy somewhat and reduce the chance of water coming on board, but their main use is in varying the appearance of the hull, by visually altering the sheerline. On small motorsailers bulwarks are unlikely to be more than a foot deep, and they are rarely used on larger motorsailers where the proportions of the hull are better. Their use is generally restricted to the motor-oriented type where they recall the fishing vessel origins (1.5). Where they are fitted, they are usually combined with a single wire lifeline which certainly produces a more secure arrangement. Gaps must be left between the bulwarks and the deck amidships so that any solid water which comes on board will be cleared rapidly. Water trapped on deck by the bulwarks could temporarily raise the centre of gravity and have a detrimental effect on stability.

By the same token, any motorsailer cockpit should be self-draining. Water that drains into the bilges can be pumped out, which is not a particularly good idea but at least gets any trapped water low down in the boat. The alternative is to have the cockpit sole above the waterline and fit drains between the sole and the outside of the hull which are of adequate size to get rid of any water quickly, even if the cockpit is filled. The cockpits found on many motorsailers can hold a ton or more of water, and it is not difficult to imagine the effect of such additional weight. Apart from stability problems, the boat is lowered bodily in the water and the chances of another wave coming on board are increased; great strain is put on any doors or washboards between green water and the interior. There is also the question of the free water surface. Water in a container such as a cockpit has a free surface and so will find its own level. Under the sort of conditions where the cockpit is more or less filled the boat will be rolling and the momentum of this water moving to and fro will accentuate the rolling with possibly damaging consequences. The same problem occurs in fuel and water tanks when they are only partly full, but there surging is much reduced by baffles.

To drain water away rapidly the drain pipes should be of a large diameter, somewhere around 3–4 in each. Unfortunately, this size is rarely fitted and the normal drains are between 1 and 2 in in diameter, fine for getting rid of spray, but bound to take a long time to cope with any heavy water. The result would be that it would get down into the bilges via the cockpit lockers, or the wheelhouse door if this was on the same level as the cockpit.

Any possibility of water finding its way down inside the hull is undesirable. After all, one of the purposes of the deck and super-structure is to keep water out. Ideally all access to the inside of the hull should be watertight, but achieving this is expensive, and can make life on board uncomfortable. A compromise has to be reached depending on the use of the boat; where it could be ex-posed to very rough conditions, trickles of water finding their way below will be a nuisance, but are unlikely to affect the safety. What is required is adequate strength in the closures of all openings to withstand the onslaught of seas or the weight of solid water.

Wheelhouse doors and cockpit locker hatches should be reasonably well fitting, but they must be strong enough to stand up to the impact of waves. I mentioned above the desirability of being able to open up the wheelhouse in fine weather, but doors which allow this will prove vulnerable in heavy weather, and

---

3.2   Both boats have a large raised cockpit accessible from the main saloon or after cabin. The upper photo is of the boat shown in (2.5) and the height of the cockpit sole is very apparent. The entire accommodation is within the hull under a flush deck, whereas in the lower picture the cockpit is somewhat deeper, with higher sides which are continuous forward and aft with the coachroof. Both main and after cabins employ a coachroof to obtain full head and foot room; the flush decks of the upper example are achieved with very high topsides. (Coronado 35, Nicholson 42)

need means of stiffening and securing them if they are to be strong enough. With motorsailers (like other yachts) spending most of their time at sea in fair weather from choice, and bad weather never being consciously sought, it is small wonder that they are largely designed for fine weather.

Assuming that the cockpit lockers are reasonably watertight and that their lids are secured so they will not float off, the wheelhouse door or companionway hatch provides the first defence against the sea. If the wheelhouse is not totally enclosed, then that much more attention will have to be given to the design of the hatch giving access to the accommodation down below, so that it is wholly capable of keeping. water out. Similarly, if the engine hatches are fitted within such a shelter or in an open cockpit they should be secured so that they will not float off or open.

A totally enclosed wheelhouse is a sort of no-man's land between the accommodation down below and the sea outside. An owner should decide where his main line of defence is to be, the choice being between the outer wheelhouse door (and indeed the whole structure) and the inner access to the accommodation. The answer would appear to be obvious, but if it were only the outer door it would be simple. Wheelhouses on motorsailers have large areas of glass to give good vision all round and these can be as vulnerable as the door in rough weather – more so, in fact, as they face forward and sideways where they are more liable to impact. This vulnerability is recognized by the fitting of toughened glass, but this is only as tough as the frames in which it is set, or their attachment to the structure. All in all, a wheelhouse can be vulnerable, and the accommodation access and engine hatches should be of adequate quality and design to serve as a second line of defence.

A fully enclosed wheelhouse is normally considered to be a dry area in a boat, but it should be designed and finished to withstand a certain amount of water. It may be necessary to have a window open to get proper visibility in bad conditions, and wet oilskins can drip a lot of water about. The interior finish should be able to stand up to this water, but the main sufferers are likely to be electrical and electronic equipment. If this is mounted high up it will be kept out of the way of most water flying about, and this is practical with most equipment except radar. Dashboard instruments and switches do not have to be mounted just forward of the wheel; they are just as conveniently placed if they are in a panel on the deckhead and are far less likely to affect the compass. With the possibility of water in small quantities entering the wheelhouse it would also be useful to fit a small drain at deck level which can run into the bilges.

A closed wheelhouse does restrict visibility and it should be possible to open windows when necessary. One on each side and one forward should be sufficient, and of course these opening windows can cool and ventilate when the weather is fine. Vision at night is affected by any lights in the wheelhouse which reflect against the windows: all lights should be capable of being covered or switched off, and this particularly applies to indicator lights in radios and other electronic equipment. Visibility is important, particularly in bad weather and for pilotage or when entering strange harbours, but it does conflict with the requirement to keep dry. Windscreen wipers and clear-view screens can help by clearing small areas, but do not provide a complete answer. The area cleared by a clear-view screen is very limited and only enables one to see over a limited arc of the horizon. Windscreen wipers are better, but they must be of a type designed for the marine environment. So often one sees car-type wipers fitted which stop working at their first contact with sea water. Wipers do smear when dealing with salt spray or small quantities of water and fresh water washers can be used to clean the screen, as on cars.

The relative merits of an enclosed wheelhouse, a steering shelter or an open steering position are largely matters for personal taste, and preferences tend to relate to the age of the owner and the use to which he puts the boat. No one of these meets all requirements and motorsailers, particularly the larger ones, often have dual steering positions. One wheel is fitted in an enclosed wheelhouse giving protection in cold or rough weather and on long passages, and the other is in the cockpit or over the wheelhouse for fine weather use or when entering or leaving harbour when good visibility is required (1.5). Such an installation does leave the owner the choice at any particular time, rather than having to make up his mind when he buys the boat. The extent to which the wheelhouse also contains part of the accommodation varies from boat to boat, and some possible arrangements are illustrated in Chapter 7.

The open steering position (3.2, 3.3) gives full visibility when sailing, and many yachtsmen find a wheelhouse or shelter restricting as they cannot see the sails properly, particularly when closehauled. In an effort to improve this situation, many builders fit a window in the roof of the wheelhouse or shelter which does bring the mainsail into view (3.1), but obviously it cannot give the same clear view as an open steering position. Weather protection and visibility just do not go together.

The question of good visibility cannot be overemphasized, both for collision avoidance in all weathers and for watching the sea in bad weather. Often one hears yachtsmen criticizing 'big ship men' for not keeping a good lookout, and of not being aware of small boats. I have been on big ships and small, and I would suggest that yachtsmen are generally much more lax in keeping a lookout. Much of this is simply due to bad layouts, and of wheelhouses in particular. With the comparatively slow speed of the motorsailer it is important to consider the view astern. It is surprising how quickly a faster vessel can catch up without being noticed.

Many hours will be spent in the wheelhouse or shelter while on passage. Similarly, in harbour the crew tend to congregate in the wheelhouse as it offers a view of what is going on around the boat. The question of seating has to be considered as it can be very tiring standing all the time. Certainly the helmsman deserves a seat, if only to locate him securely in rough weather so that he can give his full attention to controlling the boat. The dictates of space in harbour and access to the engine compartments will often mean

---

3.3 A more pronounced version of several features of current motorsailers. The central accommodation space is enclosed by a very prominent superstructure in which the profile and window arrangement begin to resemble those of power cruisers. There is a large after cabin where space has been maximized by having a long raised after deck and wide transom – seen from the quarter, the power cruiser form is very apparent. The raised cockpit is enclosed by very high sides and at its forward end runs into the cabin top, somewhat as in (5.3) and (7.2). In terms of proportions, the cabin top and sailing instruments are at about the same height above deck as the sheerline is from the water; for an adult standing on the side deck amidships, the cabin top is at waist level. (Finnrose 45)

that the helmsman's seat has to be capable of being folded away. This also gives the choice of sitting or standing at the wheel, but folding seats by their very nature are often of flimsy construction and do not give good support. In rough seas when the boat is moving about a lot, the strain on a seat can be greatly increased.

If a seat is to be really useful it should locate the occupant adequately against the movements of the boat, leaving him both hands free for the wheel and engine controls. If a boat is to be controlled properly the wheel should not become a handhold to prevent the helmsman being thrown about: his seat should perform this function. A well designed seat should incorporate arm rests for sideways location, and foot rests so that one can brace against pitching, and to prevent fatigue.

The other seating requirements in the wheelhouse are not so critical and usually take the form of a settee; any seating should offer a view out of the windows if possible. If the chart table is in the wheelhouse and has a seat, it should be designed similarly to that for the helmsman so that the navigator is left with both hands free. Where seating does not provide good location of the body, plenty of handholds should be provided and something to brace the feet against. There is nothing more tiring than trying to hold on in a seat with inadequate grips. On a long passage this can put quite a strain on the crew, and lead to bad tempers and similar evils.

When seats are not provided due to lack of space, the need for handholds is still there. Not only must they be adequate and strong, but they must be in the right places. If the boat is moving about at all violently, a person can put a surprisingly high strain on a handhold in trying to prevent himself being thrown around. A handhold which is not reliable is dangerous and trying, and careful attention must be paid to the fastenings. New boats are in the main poorly equipped with handholds, and many of those that are fitted cannot be gripped properly. The trend seems to be appearance first and function second. It is left to the owner to fit his own handholds, which is not a bad thing, because at least he can get them where he wants them. It is worth spending some time in finding the right places because they can make life on board so much more comfortable, and moving about so much safer. One of the best types is a vertical pole in the centre of the wheelhouse which can be both held and leant against, but does hinder free passage unless the space is quite large.

Handholds on deck are equally important, and it must be possible to get one's hand right around the grip. In designing and placing handholds it is as well to remember that you may have to support your whole weight from the grip. The feet and legs can help a great deal in locating the body; though they cannot grip, they can be used to brace oneself and advantage should be taken of this. Bulwarks are very helpful on deck, but failing this a toerail, which is a raised edge to the deck one or two inches high, can help. This is a fairly standard finish to the edges of decks, and also helps to prevent anything dropped from going straight over the side.

Safety on deck can be greatly enhanced by a suitable anti-slip deck covering. This is commonly used on motorsailers where the emphasis is more on quality and practicality than appearance. Good deck coverings are both heavy and expensive, but the added security they give is worth it. In the interests of economy, the covering is sometimes fitted only to the areas of deck most used. Alternatives are to mould in a roughened surface on a fibreglass deck moulding. This works well when the boat is new, but as it gets older the rough surface gradually wears smooth, and the small indentations fill up with dirt. There is little that can be done to restore the roughness except to cement some anti-slip covering over it. Special anti-slip paints can be applied to deck surfaces: their useful life is also limited, but the surface can be restored by a further application. Wooden decks are very attractive and have reasonable anti-slip properties, but they do require a fair bit of maintenance. For the owner spending a lot of time on board this may not be much of a problem, but for the weekend sailor it can be a considerable burden.

In laying out the deck space the location of the fillers for both fuel and water has to be considered. To the uninitiated this would seem to present no problems, but a poor installation can lead to water in the fuel, or vice versa, or fuel all over the deck and perhaps in the cockpit. The filler must stop any sea water which will flow over the deck from entering the tank, which demands a watertight cap; a slightly raised filler can help so that water and dirt will not collect around the cap. To prevent spillages when filling, the only satisfactory way is to have a specially constructed funnel which will screw into the thread of the filler pipe. This will not only reduce the chances of spillage, but also catch any fuel blown back up the pipe when the tank is nearly full and the venting is not adequate. Such a funnel also allows water to be flowing on deck around the filler so that any spillage is immediately washed away, or the decks to be wetted thoroughly before fueling begins.

Water tank fillers are better placed at a higher part of the deck than the fuel fillers, and well away from them so that there is no chance of contamination. Fuel and water are often taken on board at the same time (and in a hurry) and there must not be any chance of them mixing. The fuel filler is best placed at the lowest part of the deck with a scupper close by so that any spillage will drain straight overboard. Any deck covering and its adhesive around the fuel filler should be fuel-proof as far as possible. Fuel hoses for boats come in all shapes and sizes, and the filler opening should be as large as possible – cruising boats often have to use the same pipes and nozzles as working craft. By the same token, air must be able to escape from the tanks as quickly as fuel is put in, and the tank vents should be large enough to prevent blow-back.

In the interests both of ventilation and as a secondary exit from the accommodation in the event of fire, a hatch is invariably fitted on the foredeck or in the forward end of the coachroof. It also provides a quick method of getting headsails on or off the deck. This forehatch is in an exposed position and traditionally is a constant source of leaks, particularly as it is exposed to green water when the going is rough. Careful design and construction are required if such a hatch is to be satisfactory, but modern materials can now achieve this. Obviously the hatch should be completely watertight when closed, and it must be possible to open it quickly and easily from the inside to meet the fire escape requirement. Modern hatches often have a large part of their area fitted with a clear plastic insert to give more light below: this plastic must be protected as far as possible from being scratched, and its slipperiness reduced.

3.4 Rather cluttered decks which result from trying to fit too much into too little space. (Pelagian)

Any hatch must be kept unobstructed both at sea and in port if it is to fulfil its function as an escape hatch. With heavy demands on all available deck space, the hatch often ends up as being the only convenient space on which to stow the liferaft or dinghy. This temptation must be resisted, and the use of deck space carefully planned. The foredeck of a motorsailer can be very exposed in bad weather and is not a good place to stow anything unless it can be very well secured. The only thing which has a place on the foredeck is the anchor, but even this is now often carried in specially designed fairleads in which it is automatically stowed as it is hauled up.

Stowage on the after deck will depend very much on the configuration. If there is an aft cockpit stowage space will be restricted largely to lockers in the cockpit, but these are usually generous. An after cabin will sometimes have a second hatch as well, but this will be more for light and ventilation rather than as a fire escape. The top of this cabin can make a good stowage for a liferaft or radar (8.1).

Apart from the windows in the wheelhouse, the deck and superstructure have to accommodate windows and ventilators to provide light and air down below. In considering these it is important that the watertight integrity of the hull is maintained, and any windows or portholes should be small in area, strong, and adequately fastened to the hull or deck. From a safety aspect they should be of the non-opening type, so that there is no chance of them being left open at sea, but this has to be balanced against the amenities of living on board. It is common practice in fibreglass superstructures for fixed windows to be inserted using a special rubber extrusion to join the two together. This makes a quick and simple fitting, but I would question the amount of pressure from the outside that such a window could stand. All such windows should have a metal frame or have the glass on the outside so that it overlaps the surround. Pressure from outside will then tend to help to hold the window in place.

There has been considerable emphasis on safety in this chapter – perhaps too much, you may think. Remember, however, that a motorsailer is capable of extended sea passages and is thus more likely to meet all sorts of weather conditions without the benefit of shelter near at hand. Safety at sea largely depends on attention to detail: it is rarely that the large items, such as the hull, fail. Safety is largely a personal thing and it is up to each owner to decide on his own level of safety when he goes to sea, but he must also remember his responsibility towards his crew. The sea is a hard taskmaster, and long hard experience gradually teaches one caution.

Whereas hulls are shaped to meet heavy seas, superstructures tend to present rather blunt or flat areas. Under normal circumstances seas should not affect the superstructure, but abnormal circumstances are found all too often at sea and the superstructure must be built to meet any demands likely to be placed on it. Because it is not a homogeneous material like the hull but is made up of many different materials and components extra care must be taken in its design. The motor-oriented motorsailer still retains the higher, squarer lines of its ancestors, but the sailing-oriented boats are showing lower sleeker lines which are less squarely exposed to the sea. This enables the sail plan to be kept lower, improving both appearance and efficiency.

The superstructure of a motorsailer probably gives an observer the first clue to its identity and characterizes the boat. It also presents one of the most difficult areas of compromise in deciding on what should be inside and what outside. Clever design has produced many answers from both a practical and an aesthetic point of view.

4 Engines

In my experience, the engines fitted to cars usually run very reliably while those fitted to boats do not. There must be a reason for this, as basically the engines are the same except that car engines are generally petrol and boat engines diesel. Yet if anything, this should make the boat more reliable. The reason, I think, lies in the installation. Cars are mass-produced and the engine installation is thoroughly tried and tested, and all of the little unexpected snags have been ironed out. Installations in boats are more on a one-off basis, and even though established practice is followed, the unexpected snags only get found out during use at sea.

It could be argued that the engine is not critical to a motorsailer: if it does not work there should still be sails to fall back on. But this is not so. Frequently motorsailers and auxiliary sailing yachts are put into positions where the reliability of the engine can mean the difference between survival or disaster. Working close inshore or in harbour entrances are examples. If for no other reason than to ensure the owner's peace of mind, an engine should be as reliable as possible.

As far as I can discover, every production motorsailer on the market has a diesel engine. In fact it would be almost fair to say that one of the essential criteria in classifying a boat as a motorsailer is such an engine. The diesel has an inherent reliability not found in petrol engines, as it does not depend on electricity to *keep* running. Electricity and sea water do not mix, and the less one has to depend on the former the better. Diesels found in motor-sailers range from one to six cylinders depending largely on the power requirements. The four-cylinder engine is probably the most popular in the 30–40 ft range. The multi-cylinder engine produces less vibration and a more even noise which makes life on board more comfortable – an important consideration where the engine may be in use for long periods at a time.

Many production yachts are built for an international market, to widen the field for sales. If boats are to be sold in several countries it must be possible for the engine to be serviced and spares to be obtained there. Not all engine manufacturers provide a comprehensive international service, and the choice of engines for motorsailers is generally restricted to those that do. With more and more owners taking their boats to foreign countries every year, engine manufacturers are aware of this need and the service provided abroad is improving.

The importance of the engine means that the installation must be considered from the outset, and not just fitted into a convenient space as often appears to be the case. The modern diesel engine is a compact unit, but the space required for its installation does require a certain amount of vertical height and the logical place to achieve this is under the wheelhouse or cockpit floor, where the deck level has to be raised to give visibility. This position is chosen almost without exception and it has the advantage of a short, relatively horizontal propeller shaft, but it does pose problems which can only be overcome by careful design.

At sea, when the engine will often be running, the wheelhouse or cockpit will be the most popular place on the boat, where the crew will congregate when not eating or sleeping. This being the case, there must be good sound insulation between the engine compartment and the wheelhouse if conversation without shouting is to be possible. Too often this aspect is overlooked or given only perfunctory attention, but on a long passage high noise levels can prove very tiring and make the crew bad-tempered. Sound insulation should be applied to the bulkheads between the engine compartment and the cabins, particularly if there is an after cabin or a berth nearby (3.1). In this latter space, shaft and propeller noise can intrude as well. Too little attention is paid to sound insulation, which is commonly restricted just to the hatches and the deck under the wheelhouse. Good insulation is expensive, but the resulting peace and quiet is worth it. One of the problems is that the usual insulation is some type of foam, which can become very unpleasant if contaminated by engine oil or water. Non-absorbent foams are available, but another requirement is that they should be fireproof, and with all these requirements the price goes up.

Access to the engine compartment must be carefully considered. The usual answer is to provide hatches in the wheelhouse or cockpit floor, and in harbour these will give adequate access, but they will make soundproofing more difficult. At sea loose hatches are not very secure: if the boat is rolling they slide about and it is difficult to stow them adequately. In the event of a knockdown or capsize, they could simply fall off. Whether access is required for a routine inspection or because of some defect, it will still be necessary to steer, and so often removing the engine hatches can make this difficult or almost impossible. Yet by maintaining a steady course, the motion of the boat can be much reduced and life made more pleasant for those working below.

Access to the engine at sea will vary from boat to boat, and is often ignored or at least given very low priority. If at all possible, the hatches should be away from the steering position, and they should be hinged so that when lifted they can be securely fastened back. While hatches in the wheelhouse floor are inevitable, it is often possible to provide a door in one of the engine compartment bulkheads which can be used for access from inside when carrying out routine visual checks at sea. Another way of doing this is to fit a bulkhead window and a powerful light in the compartment. This way nothing has to be opened, and it is very reassuring to be able to glance at the engine every now and then.

In motorsailers with a closed wheelhouse there is no difficulty in protecting the engine from sea water. Where the wheelhouse is open-ended or where the engine is fitted under the cockpit sole, it must be additionally protected. If hatches are fitted in the sole these must be watertight and hinged so that they prevent any water coming on board from finding its way down below, and fastened down so that they cannot be opened by a knockdown.

Sea water will rapidly attack and corrode many parts of an engine, particularly the electrical fittings, and lead to a generally unhealthy dampness in the confined compartment.

A diesel engine requires large quantities of air to run efficiently; it serves the dual purpose of supporting combustion and cooling the engine compartment. The air required by the engine should be as cool as possible for maximum efficiency; however, motorsailers' engines are not normally highly tuned and this requirement is not critical. Most yacht designers have their own ideas about air intakes, and the general tendency seems to be to disguise them as anything but what they are. The usual position is on either side of the wheelhouse, but wherever they are they should prevent the ingress of water and spray as far as possible. This will only be partially successful, as there can be quite a suction on engine air intakes and some spray will inevitably be sucked in. To minimize the harm done down below, the bottom of the air intake should be positioned well away from the engine or any equipment, so that any water will find its way directly into the bilges.

Engine compartments can never be made large enough, but the conflicting demands on space within the hull mean that this area suffers. It should be possible to see and reach all parts of the engine(s) and transmission for cleaning and servicing: it will only be carried out regularly and properly if it can be done easily. Keeping the engine and its compartment clean will help to indicate faults before they become serious. Regular servicing and maintenance will go a long way to ensuring that an engine runs reliably at sea.

There seems little advantage in fitting twin engines except in the largest motorsailers. The propellers will offer more drag and the engines will be mounted higher in the hull; it should be possible for the propellers to work more efficiently in less turbulent water, but this will be more than offset by the higher initial cost. Any boat so fitted would be very much motor-oriented and unlikely to have a good performance under sail. In larger motorsailers, however, there may be some merit in a twin engine installation if only to improve the handling under power when manoeuvring.

The usual underwater shape of a motorsailer allows the engine to be mounted low down on the centreline with the propeller shaft nearly horizontal. At this angle the propeller gives maximum efficiency, and the engine and gearbox lubrication systems have the best chance of operating efficiently. Most marine engines are designed to run at angles of up to 15° from the horizontal in the fore-and-aft direction, the limiting factor being the maintenance of suction to the oil pump from the sump. This angle has to take pitching into account, so the steeper the angle of installation the less the latitude for pitching.

In the interests of reducing noise and vibration, most motorsailer installations have the engine flexibly mounted on its bearers. The advantages of reducing noise and vibration are only gained at the expense of added complication, however. If the engine can move slightly on its mountings, then all of the connections between the engine and the fixed parts of the boat have to be flexible to allow for this movement. These include controls, fuel lines, water connections, electrical connections, couplings and the propeller shaft. The introduction of these flexible connections will reduce reliability unless they are carefully engineered and installed.

Diesel engines themselves are very reliable these days, and rarely is failure due to a part of an engine actually failing. It is much more likely to be caused by one of the accessories. Apart from those actually attached to the engine, these are generally tailored to suit the individual boat, and as such can be regarded as one-off components, mainly associated with the fuel, cooling water and electrical systems. Great care must be taken with all such ancillary systems if a truly reliable installation is to be had, and nothing must be left to chance.

For seagoing use one should aim at self-sufficiency; assistance can be difficult to find and one cannot carry a complete set of spares. By careful design it is possible to provide duplication of the essential systems so ensuring greater reliability, and it could be argued that this is already done in the broad sense in the case of the motorsailer. If this principle is carried over to the engine systems then one has a good chance of not being caught out at sea.

A constant supply of clean, uncontaminated fuel is essential to the operation of any engine. The fuel system is probably the greatest area of failure in diesels, and by fitting a really reliable system one is cutting the chances of failure by at least half. A lot can be done by making sure that the fuel is at least fairly clean before it even gets into the tanks, by only taking fuel from a reliable source. If there is the slightest doubt about the cleanliness of the fuel (and one cannot always be particularly fussy as refuelling points are often few and far between) it should be passed through a fine filter before it enters the tanks.

Where practical, fuel should be carried in two separate tanks, only one of which is drawn from at a time. If one tank does prove to be contaminated for any reason there is always the reserve to turn to. The piping should be arranged so that the engine can be run off either tank independently, but there should also be a cross-feed with valves between the tanks so that fuel can be transferred to adjust trim, etc. In a twin engine installation it should be possible to run either or both engines off either or both tanks, which involves more complicated piping. All of the valves in the system should be readily accessible, preferably without having to lift the engineroom hatches.

A 70 h.p. diesel engine will use around 3 Imp gal (3.6 US gal or 13.6 litres) per hour when run at full power, but for normal cruising one can expect it to use about 2 Imp gal (2.4 US gal or 8 litres) per hour. This size of engine would be suitable for powering a motorsailer of around 6 to 8 tons displacement, so one is thinking in terms of a fuel consumption of about 0.2 Imp gal (0.24 US gal or 0.8 litre) per ton displacement per hour. Going back to the 70 h.p. engine, a fuel capacity of say 150 Imp gal (180 US gal or 6,810 litres) would give a range of over 500 miles which should be considered as the right sort of figure. Many boats carry more, and if the space can be found this is all to the good because nothing spoils cruising more than to have to be continually refuelling.

If this same 150 Imp gal capacity is distributed between two tanks each one will hold around 700 lb (320 kg) when full. These weights have to be carefully placed in the hull having regard to the trim, bearing in mind that they may be either full or empty. If they are in the bottom the effect on stability of emptying them must be considered, as the centre of gravity will be raised. Tanks on the centreline will only affect the fore-and-aft trim (as well as the height of the C G), while if they are placed on each side of the boat they will affect the transverse trim which is more critical. Side tanks will have less effect on the stability as they will be close to the centre of gravity and emptying or filling them will not move the centre of gravity appreciably. They do, however, allow the boat to be compensatingly trimmed if she has a list or an unbalanced load for any reason.

Tanks can be of either metal or fibreglass. The latter are usually formed as an integral part of the hull, but metal tanks must be firmly secured to prevent any movement. All tanks should be fitted with a manhole to give access to the interior for inspection and cleaning. This is particularly important to tanks fitted in the bottom of the boat where it is not possible to fit a sump and drain valve to drain off any water or dirt which settles out of the fuel. Water can be in the fuel when it comes on board, but it also gathers in the tanks (particularly if they are metal) through condensation. Regularly draining a sample from the bottom of the tank will check on the water content, but this should only be done after the boat has been lying at rest for some time. Any solid particles will also settle in the sump and this should be cleaned out annually.

Both solid and water contamination will settle when the boat is at rest, but in a seaway the fuel slopping around in the tank will mix it up and so a small glass settling bowl is included in the fuel line before the engine. This bowl is glass so that water or dirt can be seen and removed before it reaches danger level. Because diesel engines will not tolerate any form of contamination in the fuel, a special fine filter with a replaceable element is fitted as part of the engine, and some systems include an additional filter between tanks and engine.

Going back to the fuel tanks, the fillers should be out on deck so that any spillage during filling does not run into the bilges. Breather pipes should also be led out on deck so that any fumes do not contaminate the accommodation or bilges. The ends of breathers can be simply bent over in a gooseneck if they are placed in a sheltered position; otherwise, where water may be flying about the ends must be protected with baffles or fine gauze to prevent water entering the pipe and contaminating the fuel. Breather pipes led through the hull are prone to this and are not a good idea.

The outlet pipe from any fuel tank should be fitted with a shut-off valve close to the tank, but designed for remote operation. This serves the dual purpose of stopping spillage if the pipe is damaged in any way or has to be disconnected, and as a means of shutting off fuel in the event of a fire in the engine compartment.

These valves should preferably be accessible from the deck or cockpit, which will mean extending their spindles, but this means that the fuel can be shut off without having to go below.

Fuel supply lines from the tank to the engine should be carefully routed to avoid places where they might get crushed, knocked or chafed. Metal pipes are preferred, but plastic is acceptable provided it is of a type specified as suitable for the purpose. Metal and plastic piping may crack or melt in the event of a fire, hence the need for shut-offs, so that fuel is not added to the fire. In routeing plastic or metal piping it should be kept well clear of hot exhaust pipes. With a flexibly mounted engine part of the fuel line will have to be flexible to allow for movement and should be a length of the special flexible metal piping made for the purpose. Plastic piping is not suitable as it is liable to harden and crack.

With some types of diesel engine a return fuel pipe has to be fitted from the engine to the tank to return excess fuel not passed through the injectors. This should be engineered to the same high standards as the main fuel line, and will be equally affected by vibration. You cannot take too much trouble with a fuel system. When the engine can be run off alternate tanks, account must be taken of the fact that the return pipe may only return the fuel to one tank. This can give an apparent unexpectedly high fuel consumption, and the tanks will have to be changed over earlier than expected.

Cooling systems are a necessary evil associated with diesel engines to carry away the waste heat. Because they circulate raw sea water through a series of pipes, any leak can start to fill the boat with water. It thus becomes another of the critical systems associated with the engine, and demands care and attention in its design and execution. Water cooling systems come in two types, one where the raw sea water circulates through the engine and directly cools it and the other where a closed fresh water system cools the engine, the fresh water being cooled by sea water via a heat exchanger. In spite of its added complexity, the latter system is coming into more general use as it gives a more stable engine temperature and reduces corrosion in the cooling water passages. It also allows antifreeze to be put into the system when the engine is used in the winter.

The raw sea water used as coolant in both systems is drawn in via a seacock in the hull and an engine-driven pump. With the engine usually mounted below the waterline, the whole system is under pressure whether the engine is running or not. By closing the seacock the system can be isolated, and the valve should be visible and readily accessible so that it can be rapidly found and turned off in the event of a leak. Ideally the valve spindle should be extended above deck level, because once flooding starts it may be difficult to locate the valve under water.

When the hull seacock is open all of the piping is under pressure, and this pressure can be increased by the motion of the boat in a seaway. In a rough sea pressure could be increased by several times its normal value by slamming, and the piping should be engineered to withstand this. Where possible metal piping should be used, but flexible sections will have to be introduced to allow for vibration and the movement of the engine. These sections of flexible piping should be of a suitably strong material, and fitted with double worm-drive clips.

To prevent foreign matter entering the cooling system it is common practice to fit a filter, which can be in the seacock casting or a separate fitting in the system. The former would seem to be the appropriate place as it stops anything even getting in. Any water filter should be capable of being easily cleaned, and in an accessible position.

After the sea water has been used to cool the engine either directly or indirectly, in most installations it is injected into the exhaust pipe to cool the hot exhaust gases. A common practice nowadays is to make the exhaust pipe from large-diameter flexible reinforced rubber piping. This makes installation much easier than for a rigid system, but such piping will catch fire fairly readily unless it is continuously cooled by injected water. The system works efficiently until the sea water circulation stops for some reason or other; a fire (and possibly flooding) is then fairly imminent, yet I have not come across a boat which is fitted with a warning device to indicate when sea water is not circulating. Raw water circulation could stop for a variety of reasons: a blockage of the inlet or filter is the most obvious, but a pipe fracturing or a water pump drive belt slipping or breaking could have the same effect. With direct sea water cooling a fairly rapid rise in temperature will result, but in all probability the smell from the burning exhaust will be the first indication, rather than the temperature gauge. Where cooling is via a heat exchanger and fresh water reservoir, engine temperature will not alter for some considerable time. All of the causes mentioned are possibilities when running at sea, particularly the first one which could be caused by plastic bags or the like. I feel that we are perhaps a little casual in our approach to the cooling system on boats.

There are two other types of cooling which do not use sea water directly. One is a closed fresh water system where the heated water from the engine is passed through tubes running outside the hull, where the sea water flowing past cools it (keel cooler). The other is direct air cooling of the cylinders. In the former system the outside tubes are vulnerable when taking the ground or to floating objects. For air cooling, large air ducts have to be accommodated to ensure that adequate air gets to the engine, and these engines have a higher noise level. Probably the main reason why they are not in more common use is because they have to be fitted with a dry exhaust.

Dry exhausts are those without water injection, and thus they have to be made of metal as they run at fairly high temperatures. They will take up more space because they cannot be run close to wood, fibreglass or inflammable fittings, and because there is no water mixed with the hot exhaust gas the exhaust is noisier. The engineering of a dry exhaust is difficult, particularly with a flexibly mounted engine, as a length of specially made flexible metal pipe has to be inserted in the system. With these problems it is easy to see how the flexible water-injected exhaust pipe has come into favour, and how the possibility of fire from this source has been conveniently overlooked.

Whatever type of exhaust system is fitted, the exhaust gases have to come out into the open air at some point. With a water-injected exhaust this is invariably through the hull, so that the water that comes out as well falls straight into the sea. This is the theory at least, but if the exhaust should be on the windward side a lot of the somewhat oily water will blow back on board. On the leeward side the exhaust gases are often wafted back to the boat by the wind eddies around the hull. The same thing can happen when the exhaust outlet is at the stern, but this is the position usually chosen, with the opening placed just above the waterline under the counter or cruiser stern. The exhaust pipe is led up just under the deck before dropping to the opening, to prevent water running back.

The electrical system on a diesel-powered boat is not essential once the engine is running. However it is now considered essential for starting the engine owing to the sad demise of the starting handle, and the use of larger engines than formerly. The handle did make the engine completely independent of electrics, and on some engines can still be obtained as an extra. With others there is no question of hand starting, because of the difficulty of turning the engine over. (One can't help feeling that the main reason why starting handles are no longer fitted to motorsailers' engines is lack of space in which to fit and operate the handle.) On this basis the electrical system is important, and for other reasons. Navigation lights are now all electrical and these must be available for use at all times. Fresh water systems, now commonly fitted to ensure running fresh water at taps, rely on an electric pump; there is often no other means of getting at the water in the tanks. Some fuel systems also have electric pumps. So, having accepted that an electrical system is now essential on a modern yacht, it must be made as reliable as possible.

The first step is to ensure that sea water cannot get to any part of the system. Any components which have to be placed where they are likely to be affected by salt water or spray must be waterproof; this applies to switches and junction boxes as well as the actual fittings themselves. Waterproofing electrical equipment makes it expensive, so wherever possible these fittings will be placed where they are protected. One has to be careful in this, as places such as the instrument panels and controls can be contaminated by salt water dripping off wet oilskins, etc. There is not a need for full waterproofing here, but some form of protection is necessary.

Alternators are now common on marine diesels and they can provide a fairly high charging rate to compensate for the high demands sometimes put on the electrical supply. Naturally an alternator will only charge the batteries when the engine is running, and some of the highest demands for electricity can be made in harbour or at anchor. Water pumps, lighting and refrigeration can provide a constant drain which may leave the battery too weak to start the engine the next morning. A battery will give little indication that it is running low until it is too low to provide enough power for starting, because that requires significantly more current than other uses.

The demand for electrical power when in harbour is now fully recognized. It provides the convenience of home living which is demanded nowadays on boats, and there are several methods of ensuring adequate supply, such as fitting an auxiliary generator. It is not difficult to find the space, but the main objection is the noise it creates. Boats in harbour are generally peaceful objects, and you will not endear yourselves to those in adjacent berths or across the anchorage if you keep your auxiliary running all evening; it's not very pleasant for those on board, either. A lot of marinas now make provision for an electrical supply to be plugged in when berthed alongside, which is a simple way of meeting the boat's power requirements. The electricity can be used directly at its supply voltage if suitable equipment and circuits are installed on board, or reduced and rectified to provide DC power at the normal voltage of the boat's supply. The latter is the best arrangement as all of the equipment on board can be used as designed, and it obviates the need for two separate circuits and reduces high voltages with their added problems to a minimum. The transformer and rectifier (or converter) unit are fairly compact and can be installed in a suitably dry compartment.

A third solution to the problem of power supplies is now commonly found; it involves having two batteries, both of which are charged from the alternator via what is termed a blocking diode between the two batteries. One battery is then used solely for engine starting while the other supplies all of the auxiliary circuits. By this means there will always be power in the starting battery even though the auxiliary battery is completely exhausted, assuming that its charge has been maintained.

To ensure that the batteries are being charged properly when under way, a charging meter should be fitted among the instruments, and also a battery selector switch. A slipping drive belt or a broken wire can reduce the amount of charge considerably and in consequence the power being used will not be replaced. Broken wires are usually caused by the movement of the engine on its mountings when it is flexibly mounted: the continual flexing of the wire can cause fatigue failure, and this is particularly the case with the main battery leads to and from the starter motor. A failure in these wires could also cause sparking which could lead to fire. All wiring should be securely clipped up, and positioned where it is unlikely to get knocked, chafed or snagged.

Wiring circuits in boats should always be of the two-wire variety, not employing the hull or engine as a return path. Electrical currents flowing in this manner can accentuate the problem of electrolytic corrosion. In a similar manner, the leakage of current to earth should be avoided as this can cause considerable deterioration in the hull of a wooden boat, where the damp wood can offer a path for such currents with resultant corrosion of metal fastenings or sterngear. These problems are not so acute on the modern fibreglass boat, but care and attention with wiring is still necessary. An isolating switch for each battery will enable all the wiring to be disconnected when the boat is not in use and will prevent rundown due to poor insulation or damp causing current leakage.

Batteries are heavy items and should be securely fastened into the boat, but at the same time kept accessible so that they will get the care and attention they require. Batteries should be placed in stout lead-lined or plastic trays so that any acid spillage will be contained, and secured against any movement. This means holding them down in the tray as well as tight sideways location: remember, they may be dumped out by a broach, a knockdown, or rolling over. Movement will mean flexing of the connecting wires (at least) and will eventually lead to failure.

In a marine environment one cannot take too much trouble with the electrical system. It is a pity that most marine diesel engines show their road vehicle ancestry by having the starter motor mounted low down by the crankcase where it is more liable to be soaked by water from the bilges.

We have seen the need for a charging indicator and for some indication of the sea water flow for the cooling system, among the instruments. Engine oil pressure and water temperature gauges are usually standard, and are sometimes supplemented by similar gauges for the gearbox, water temperature being replaced by oil temperature. Gauges can often help in the detection of problems before serious harm is done to the engine: they do, however, demand that someone is watching them if they are to be of any value. This is not always the case on a yacht where an autopilot is used. As there is no longer a need for anyone to be positioned at the wheel the gauges are less likely to be scanned frequently. While the necessity for visual indicators remains, there is a requirement for some form of audible warning device which will sound off when a pre-set temperature or pressure is reached. Whatever the crew are doing, and they could well be on deck adjusting sail, such a device is not easy to ignore. A second-best system is warning lights, but these are usually too dim to be seen easily during the day, and unlikely to be seen from the galley or the deck.

Where the engine may be run for prolonged periods, as when motorsailing, one of the likely causes of a drop in oil pressure is lack of oil in the sump. It is a fairly simple matter to check the level with the dip stick, but not so easy to top up the oil when the boat is rolling in a seaway. An improvement which can make the job easier is a tank mounted high in the engine compartment with a pipe leading to the rocker box cover. The tank is filled with engine lubricating oil before starting a passage and then it is a simple matter to open a valve in the pipe to allow the oil to flow into the engine.

Directly checking the engine when running at sea should be routine every few hours. Those parts which are likely to want checking or attention should be made as accessible as possible, when they are more likely to receive the attention they deserve. No one likes crawling about in an engine compartment at sea, and things should be made as easy as possible. Similarly, regular servicing, whether you do this yourself or entrust it to the boat-yard, is much more likely to be done thoroughly and conscientiously if it can be done easily.

Gearboxes come in for little comment. In general they run reliably and require little attention other than oil changes. Types of gearbox vary and some offer advantages. One type, perhaps anticipating a failure of the operating mechanism, ensures that the ahead gear can be engaged in the event of a failure. This at least gets you home, but with efficient sails, may not be absolutely essential. With the large propellers fitted to most motorsailers, engine speed has to be reduced so that the propeller operates at optimum speed. Some gearboxes incorporate reduction gears, while in other cases a separate reduction gearbox has to be fitted. The latter system does offer the advantage of lowering the propeller shaft line so that it can be more nearly horizontal.

Cost is a large factor in determining the quality of an engine installation. A cheap or awkward installation is liable to give trouble at some time, and it is as well to remember that a reliable engine represents a far better safety factor than all the flares, liferafts and other safety equipment put together. From a more mundane point of view, a reliable engine represents peace of mind and more enjoyable cruising.

The engine installation in a motorsailer has to stand very different treatment to that on a motor cruiser. Motorsailers are prone to all the nasty things that can happen to sailing boats, such as being knocked down or swamped by waves. Cockpits can and do fill with water, and all these things can be to the detriment of the engine installation just at a time when it may be most needed. Air intakes should be protected with good baffles, water must not get into the fuel tanks, and above all, everything – tanks, batteries, ducting, hoses, wiring, generators – must be firmly secured. Another fact worth remembering when looking at a motorsailer's installation is that the engine may have to run for many hours when the boat is heeled at a sharp angle. The oil sumps of most marine diesel engines will take this quite happily provided that the sump is kept full; however, marinized car or truck units may not be designed for prolonged use at an angle. Problems may also occur when the intake for cooling water is not close to the keel: with the boat heeled, the intake may become uncovered and the engine overheat. One could fit two intakes (one on each side), but inevitably the changeover would be forgotten, and locating the intake as near as possible to the lowest part of the hull is preferable.

5 Rigs

Designing a motorsailer that will sail well is not an easy task. The hull form is usually not primarily designed for sailing performance and has greater resistance than would otherwise be the case. There are usually limitations on the size of both mast(s) and sails in the interests of easy handling, and things must be kept simple. It sounds impossible, yet most modern motorsailers sail moderately well, and some extremely well. Almost without exception they can provide enjoyable sailing.

How is this possible? I suppose it depends to a certain extent on what is regarded as enjoyable sailing. If you are intent on sailing a boat at its maximum all the time, then the answer is a racing boat. On the other hand, reasonable progress having regard to the wind conditions prevailing is possible in a motorsailer.

An average motorsailer of around 35 ft overall will have a maximum speed of about $7\frac{1}{2}$ knots as a displacement hull. Doubling the power available will produce hardly any increase in speed once this maximum has been reached. Racing yachts spend a lot of time and money in trying to find a lot of extra power to gain a little extra speed, because they are working near their maximum. Lower down the scale, a reduction in the available power by say a half from what is required to achieve the maximum will still give good performance, and for the 35 ft hull in question should still give speeds of over 6 knots. This can be shown when motoring: a considerable reduction in r.p.m. from that giving top speed will have little effect on the performance, providing the boat is generously powered, and usually saves a good deal of fuel.

Sailing at 6 knots in a motorsailer of average size would be considered quite adequate for most owners and can be achieved with a fairly simple rig, and sails which are not too large or heavy for two people to handle. The extra speed of which the hull is capable would be nice to have, but the additional cost and effort in handling the larger rig is not often justified or desired on a motorsailer. On a racing yacht every last ounce of speed counts and the consequences and cost speak for themselves.

In talking about maximum hull speeds, or even the reduced figure at which motorsailers usually perform, it is assumed that there is plenty of wind. With their moderate sail areas and simple, low rigs, motorsailers require a good fresh breeze to give their best performance. In light winds they will make progress, but the combination of a heavy hull and small sails is not conducive to performance: the frustration involved will almost certainly mean that most owners will start the engine. This aspect of performance in no way contradicts the definition of a motorsailer, where it is required to perform under 'adverse' weather conditions. In my experience most thrive in a strong wind, and give very enjoyable sailing. The rig should suit the cruising area.

Given that a motorsailer is fitted with a reasonably efficient sailing rig, then the power available from the sails will be more or less proportional to their area. The power required to drive a hull at a given speed can be approximately calculated from rather complex formulae, but a more accurate result can be obtained from tank-testing a model of the proposed hull. With motorsailers now being built on what almost amounts to a production line basis, tank testing is being used more and more to give reliable data before going to the expense of producing the real thing.

Having determined the power required to drive the hull at the required speed, the designer will have to work out the sail area required. It will depend on the wind strength at which maximum speed is to be attained, and this should be as low as possible. Sail can always be reduced if the wind gets stronger, but it is not so easy to increase it for light winds without additional expense and complication. A great many variable factors have to be considered: not only does the rig have to produce power over a range of wind strengths, but also on all points of sailing.

In hull design, the weight of the vessel is assumed to act through the centre of gravity (CG). Similarly with sails, the power produced is said to act through the centre of effort (CE) of the sails, and its position alters both longitudinally and transversely depending on how the sails are set. Most calculations involve the boat in its closehauled configuration, and the centre of effort then approximates to the geometric centre of the area of the sails viewed in profile. (This can be found by calculating the geometric centre of each individual sail, and then combining these in one point, having regard to the area and relative spacing of each sail.) The CE of the sails is used in two ways, first to determine the stability when closehauled and heeling. Only a small proportion of the wind's force is transmitted into forward motion, and quite a large proportion heels the boat. There must thus be an adequate righting tendency brought about by ballast and the transverse shape of the hull. The effect of the wind is self-compensating to a degree: the further over the boat heels, the less will be the effective area of the sails exposed to the wind, and also the CE will be effectively lowered. Once the boat is on her beam ends there will be no sail area exposed, but hopefully before this state is reached a position of equilibrium will be reached where the wind pressure and righting moments balance each other.

The position of the CE is also used to achieve the correct balance, and in this respect it is the fore-and-aft positions of the CE of each sail which counts. The balance largely determines how a boat steers, and if sailing is to be pleasurable then the balance must be right. We have seen how the sideways thrust of the wind on the sails heels a boat when closehauled, but this thrust also drives her bodily sideways through the water. Leeway is resisted by the underwater portion of the hull, and the centre through which it acts is called the centre of lateral resistance (CLR). This is considered to be the geometric centre of the underwater shape of the hull in profile.

If the CE of the sails and the CLR of the hull are not above each other, they will combine to produce a turning force which will tend to steer the boat. Where the CE is forward of the CLR, the boat's head will be turned to leeward, and vice versa. Either way the rudder will have to be held at an angle to compensate, if the required course is to be made good, which will increase drag. It can also prove very tiring for the helmsman and put unnecessary strain on the steering gear, and make efficient sailing difficult or impossible.

A number of factors will affect both the centre of effort and the centre of lateral resistance on any given boat, and the angle of the sails to the wind and the angle of heel are but two of them. Sufficient to say that the two centres vary both in their positions in relation to the hull and in their relation to each other. At best, their calculation is an approximation and the final adjustment is done with the rig and sails, variations in hulls being difficult to achieve, except in the case of some centreboarders or keel-centreboarders. Most designers aim to get the CE slightly aft of the centre of lateral resistance (5.1) so that in practice the boat carries a modest degree of weather helm, i.e. if left to its own devices it rounds up into the wind.

In obtaining optimum balance it may be necessary to alter the mast position or rake, or the relative areas of the sails. On a production boat it is to be hoped that all of this tuning has been carried out on the prototype and that succeeding boats benefit from this and turn out well balanced. This does not mean that the owner can forget about balance: every time he alters sail areas, either by reefing or changing sails, or shifts their CE by trimming, the balance will be altered, but if these changes are done intelligently it should be possible to retain reasonable balance. With the simple sloop rigs of most smaller motorsailers, the possible alterations are limited. Assuming that the boat is balanced when both sails are set, simply reefing the main when the wind increases will make the helm very heavy, with large rudder angles required to maintain course. A smaller jib set with a reefed main will restore balance. An alternative to putting up a smaller jib would be to reef the existing jib, if that is possible.

The general desire among most designers and owners is to have a boat which will perform efficiently under most conditions, and they are prepared to introduce and accept a degree of complication to get this. On larger motorsailers this involves splitting up the sail area, giving a more flexible sail arrangement and also

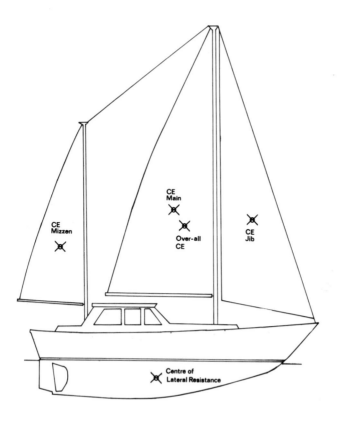

5.1

keeping the size of the sails within the limits of what can be comfortably handled by a small crew. The foretriangle can be made larger so that two headsails can be carried, either by moving the mast farther aft or by having a bowsprit so that the headstay is ahead of the stem. The latter remedy will bring the overall centre of effort well forward, and will only be acceptable on boats with a deep forefoot where the CLR will also be well forward. This shape of hull is not so common these days and is more likely to be found in the motor-oriented type of motorsailer. Moving the mast farther aft will produce a better balance with the usual shape of modern hulls. Cutter rig is not very often seen on current motorsailer designs, most having ketch rigs. That the extra cost is considered worthwhile is seen in the fact that most modern motorsailers of the larger type use this rig. However, as a corrective measure it is a very considerable step to take, as is shifting the mast.

Ketch rig offers enormous variation in balance and a logical sequence of reducing sail. The main can be reefed without altering the balance to any degree, then taken in altogether. This means that in a strong wind the largest sail has been taken down and stowed before really difficult conditions develop. The remaining sails forward and aft can be balanced easily, and are relatively easily handled if they have to be taken in or reefed. The mizzen is easily handled from the cockpit and there is no need to expose the crew on the foredeck in bad weather. For this reason it can be retained as a steadying sail under very bad conditions, knowing that it is unlikely to cause embarrassment. The mizzen will also help to keep the boat head to wind when under engine, and relieve the strain on the helmsman. The wind acting on this area of sail aft will always tend to keep the stern downwind allowing the bow to remain up into the wind.

The experienced yachtsman may scoff at the idea of all this talk of keeping sail areas small and easily handled, and lessening the risk of exposure on the foredeck. To many, one of the joys of going to sea is in accepting and meeting the challenge which large sails and strong winds give. In a motorsailer, however, the basic concept is to provide a good cruising boat which can weather bad conditions, but which in most cases can be safely handled by a crew of two, often a husband and wife team. It is not for heroics and breaking records, but a vehicle for extended comfortable cruising, and this must be remembered when talking of sail arrangements.

A lot has been said about balance, because this question of getting the sails to match the hull is a very significant aspect of any sailing boat. Most of the reports of boats being bad sailers or cranky result from bad balance (some from rigs that are just too small), and while it should have been achieved in the basic design there is still a lot that an owner can do once he has identified the problem. Balance has so far been discussed in relation to closehauled sailing or when the wind is on the beam, when there is greater sideways force. When the wind is abaft the beam a different set of circumstances arises.

There is a position about which any hull will rotate naturally in the horizontal plane when external force is applied. It will be close to or at the centre of lateral resistance, as the two ends of the boat will offer the same resistance to turning, and will be determined partly by the profile of the underwater hull, and also by its shape in cross-section. When a boat is running, the centre of effort of each sail will be more or less in line with its luff in the fore-and-aft direction, that is in line with the mainmast for the mainsail and about a third of the way up the stay for a headsail. It is important that the combined CE of the sails is ahead of the turning centre of the hull otherwise the steering will be unstable. If the centre of effort were abaft the turning centre, it would be rather like pushing a caster wheel along when it was not trailing, and steering would have to be greatly over-corrected to maintain any semblance of a course. In effect the boat would be pushed along by its sails instead of pulled. There is less chance of this occurring where a sloping forefoot ensures that the turning centre is usually aft of amidships. A ketch could get into this situation if running under mizzen alone, or possibly under main and mizzen. If sail has to be shortened when running, the after sails should be taken down first.

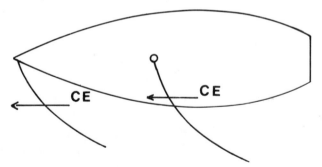

5.2

So far in this discussion the implied assumption has been that the forces acting on the sails have been over the fore-and-aft centreline of the boat. In practice the sails are always off to one side or the other so the CE is in effect offset from the centreline towards the side on which they lie. This has to be taken into account in assessing balance and steering tendency. When close-hauled this turning effect will be small as the CE will be only slightly offset to leeward. It will effectively turn the boat's head up to windward, but should be balanced or even exceeded by the added resistance of the deeply immersed side of the hull to leeward and the drag of the sails. When running the CE will be well out to leeward, particularly if headsail(s) and main are on the same side; it will also move forward (5.2). The shape of the immersed hull must be such that it balances the sails on any point of sailing, whether heeled or upright. There is little that can be done where a boat performs badly in this respect, though in some cases recutting sails (which can be costly) may help, and it is an aspect worth looking at closely when trying out an unfamiliar boat.

The final balancing of any boat under sail will be very much a matter for personal preference and can be controlled in many ways by the owner. Where he will be restricted in setting up the balance will be if the boat has only a basic set of sails. With a sloop rig where only the mainsail can be reefed, the alterations are limited, and there is little that can be done in the way of increasing performance when the wind is light. With this in mind, many designers indicate a fairly comprehensive wardrobe of sails which can be obtained as optional extras.

The owner must decide what he wants in the way of sailing from his motorsailer. If he is going to start the engine every time the wind drops to light airs, there is little point in spending large sums of money on sails. To get a reasonably complete wardrobe could add an additional 5 per cent or more to the basic cost of the boat. If one intends to spend a lot of time sailing this will be a good investment, and for reasonable light wind performance big lightweight sails such as a genoa and spinnaker are essential. It is usual for those motorsailers at the sailing end of the range to be offered with a wide variety of optional sails. The variety will also increase with overall length. The larger craft will invariably have two masts, and may be rigged as a schooner to get maximum sail area, or set a staysail between the masts.

If only one sail can be added to the wardrobe a genoa is probably the more versatile, as it can be used when both reaching and running. Spinnakers are used on motorsailers and cruisers more and more. They require a bit more handling and gear than other sails, but for the sailing enthusiast a spinnaker can give a considerable improvement in performance when the wind is abaft the beam. The mast attachments for poles (or at least the tracks) are sometimes incorporated as standard, but on other boats have to be specified when ordering. It is not so easy to fit them after a mast has been finished.

The sailing-oriented motorsailers usually have white sails, but on those modelled after traditional working craft they are frequently tan. This is purely for aesthetic purposes, as with modern synthetic sail materials there is no benefit in having sails of this colour except for appearance's sake, and there is a disadvantage in that coloured synthetics deteriorate faster from sunlight.

In order to emphasize further the traditional aspect, there was a trend to gaff mainsails like those on their working boat ancestors. Gaff rig is less efficient than Bermudan, particularly to windward, but it does keep the centre of effort of the sails lower, thus improving the stability except when running. The advantage of a shorter mast is offset by the additional weight aloft of the gaff, which in running is offset from the centreline. The gaff rig has little to offer apart from its appearance, and has now virtually died out on motorsailers.

Modern sails are made almost invariably of Terylene (Dacron) which means that little maintenance is required. However the mainsail and mizzen in particular if not stowed carefully can suffer wear due to movement when the boat is under power. Because the stitching on synthetics does not sink into the material but stands proud, it is more subject to wear than on natural fibre fabrics and must be examined at intervals.

The size of the sails carried on a particular boat is limited by its length and the height of the mast(s). Length is fixed by the original design concept, although it can be extended by a bowsprit. This is not now a common practice as a bowsprit can prove an embarrassment in crowded anchorages and marinas, and it also tends to move the centre of effort too far forward in relation to most modern hull shapes. However, on some boats the addition or lengthening of a bowsprit may improve rig balance or allow a larger area of useful sail to be set. For practical purposes the mast height for a given length of boat is governed by the sail area required. With the moderate performance accepted from many motorsailers the mast is kept at a reasonable height which in turn means that the standing rigging required is relatively simple, and the mast can be stronger for the same weight as a taller one.

With a low mast height in relation to hull length, the sails probably have what is termed a low aspect ratio (the ratio of the vertical height of a sail to its foot length). On sloop rigged motorsailers it may be around 2 in contrast to 3 or more on pure sailing boats. A high aspect ratio sail gives better windward performance and this is well worth considering when assessing the sailing capability of a motorsailer. One advantage of the ketch rig is that it can have sails of higher aspect ratios while still keeping mast heights fairly low. Generally speaking, the higher the mast(s), the higher will be the centre of effort of the sailplan with the consequent need to increase the ballast ratio to compensate. For the most comfortable cruising the centre of effort should be as low as practical. As a guide, the mast height on most motorsailers is approximately equal to the overall length of the hull. Those where emphasis is placed on sailing usually have higher masts; those with the emphasis on motoring, lower masts than this average.

Racing yachts will often have a complicated system of spreaders and shrouds, and as many as four spreaders on each side may be used. The object is to make the mast as light and as small in cross-section as possible in the quest for sailing efficiency, while bracing it against high stresses. In a motorsailer, where reliability and simplicity are the order of the day, it is rare to find more than one set of spreaders fitted, and the mast section will be of generous proportions to give a good reserve of strength; it is almost invariably an aluminium extrusion which gives a good combination of lightness and stiffness.

In cross-section, aluminium masts are usually pear-shaped or oval to give greater rigidity in the fore-and-aft direction where spreaders cannot be used. This shape is slightly less efficient as a leading edge to the sail than a round section of the same cross-sectional area, as it will present a larger area to the wind when closehauled and thus interfere more with the flow of air over the sail, but the extra stiffness is more important. Aluminium masts have to be sound deadened by applying a thin layer of suitable plastic to the inside surface of the mast, otherwise the noise of the wind on the mast and the halyards banging against it would become almost unbearable.

The racing practice of leading the halyards down through the inside of the mast is now commonly used on cruising yachts and motorsailers. By thus hiding the halyards away there is less windage and interference with the air flow over the sails as well as a cleaner, tidier appearance. There is also much less risk of the halyards getting tangled up with each other or the shrouds or crosstrees. Internal halyards are led out through sheaves either in the side of the mast or in the heel, depending largely on how it is stepped. Wire halyards are led to a halyard winch to which the end of the wire is permanently fastened; hoisting sail is then simply a matter of winding on the winch handle. This is slow in the early stages of hoisting, and for this reason rope halyards used with a halyard winch are preferred by many. With this method the sail is hoisted rapidly by hand until it becomes difficult; turns are then put on the winch and the extra leverage used to haul it up tight.

Traditionally the mast passes through the deck or coachroof and the heel fits into a socket above the keel, with the downward thrust taken by the strongest part of the hull. Disadvantages of this method are the difficulty of getting a watertight seal where the mast passes through the deck, its intrusion into the accommodation, and the difficulty in lowering the mast. The only way is to lift it out. These disadvantages have lead to the practice of stepping masts on the deck or coachroof. The downward thrust is still transmitted to the keel by means of a stanchion or pillars placed between the deck and the keel (with additional support from bulkheads), but this can be of small cross-section and it intrudes less on the accommodation, and can even make a useful handhold. On deck there may be a tabernacle, where a pin through the mast is supported on a metal structure, allowing the mast to pivot in a fore-and-aft direction for lowering. Some modern designs pivot the mast at deck level by the simple expedient of fitting what amounts to a large hinge to the heel of the mast. The hinge pin is usually easily removed once the mast is lowered so that it can be stowed level. Sheaves for the halyards can be fitted in the heel of the mast just above the hinged end fitting, and there is no tabernacle to foul their leads. Non-pivoting mast steps may be designed to allow some fore-and-aft adjustment of mast position to alter the balance of the boat.

Wooden masts are still found on some motorsailers, mainly in an attempt to maintain a traditional appearance. Wood offers little other advantage. It is becoming increasingly difficult to get suitable timber for reliable masts and the labour involved in shaping them makes them expensive. A wooden mast will be heavier

than its aluminium counterpart and require more maintenance. Appearance has to be a major factor to overcome these disadvantages.

The sailplan of most motorsailers is contained within the length of the boat, which with the low masts enables the standing rigging to be kept simple. The leads have to be carefully planned to not interfere with the sails or sheets, and so that there are no unfair or angled stresses on components. When running with the wind the mainsail, and the mizzen if any, will bear against the after shroud(s) and the spreader(s), perhaps for days. Spreaders must be carefully faired and padded to ensure that there is no chance of the sail catching or tearing, and spreader ends and shrouds covered with plastic tubing, baggywrinkle or similar material to reduce chafe and marking.

Masts and rigging on motorsailers are properly designed with a good margin of safety so that there is little chance of failure. With modern sails of synthetic fibre cloth full sail can often be left up when the wind is blowing force 6. The limiting factor is then the angle of heel which the boat assumes, remembering that leeway becomes excessive as the angle of heel increases. It is often comfort rather than safety which dictates a reduction in sail. With a good reliable engine, this is the time when many owners will switch on and take all sail off rather than go to the bother of reefing. However the steadying effect of having some sail up can make life on board so much more comfortable that reefing can be well worthwhile, and the reefed sails should still contribute usefully to powering the boat.

5.3 *Delfina*, an unusual and sophisticated 53 ft motorsailer designed by MacLear & Harris and built by the Berthon Boat Co. in 1972. The mainsail is set on a roller stay aft of the mast and loose-footed on a short boom; it can be roller-reefed electrically, as can the jib. A similar arrangement but having a longer boom with a gooseneck at the mast has been employed on other boats by the same designers (the 87 ft *Aria* has a boomless main and electric and manual gear for hoisting, furling and trimming all sails). The mast is nearly amidships, allowing large jibs with long luffs, a wide base for the shrouds, and a place for the radar scanner forward of the mast.

Roller reefing on the mainsail is commonplace on cruising yachts and with limited crews is almost essential. Even then it is a two-man job if it is to be done quickly and safely. Some motor-sailers retain the traditional reef points; they work well enough, once tied in, but tying in a reef is not an easy task in a strong wind with a limited crew. Those designs that involve the crew standing on top of the wheelhouse to reef certainly require some other system. Part of the attraction of the ketch rig lies in the possibility of effectively reducing sail by simply stowing the main, leaving the boat still balanced. Jib roller reefing can also be fitted to most boats as an optional extra, and to carry it one stage further, can be done electrically; the operation can be carried out from the cockpit, at least in theory. This is certainly easy handling, but it is an expensive arrangement, and the money can often be better spent on more pressing requirements.

Sheet leads require careful planning for sail handling and manoeuvring to be easy; and over long passages, wear and chafe should be minimized with fairleads and amply large blocks and cleats. Jib sheets must run freely if the sail is to cross from one side to the other when tacking. Setting a jib or staysail on a boom means that the size of the sail is restricted to fit within the fore-triangle or inner forestay and not foul the mast (7.3). It allows a tackle to be fitted to the end of the boom with the other end sliding on a horse across the foredeck and the sheet lead aft to the cockpit. This system enables tacking without any adjustment of the sheets and is used on some boats to simplify handling, but it does result in a slight loss of sailing efficiency as the sail shape cannot be completely controlled.

The mainsheet requires careful positioning where a wheelhouse can interfere with the lead, particularly with a ketch rig and the mainsail well forward. In some cases the sheet is led from nearer the middle of the boom down to a horse in front of the wheelhouse, but the more general arrangement is to lead it to the cockpit aft of the wheelhouse. The mainsheet is invariably a three or four part tackle and the cockpit should be clear of things on which this might foul when the boom changes sides.

With all parts of the modern mast and rigging now made of stainless steel, aluminium or plastic, there should be little to fear from corrosion and thus little maintenance is required. Shackles should be checked for tightness occasionally, and moused where possible. The vibration when motoring can quickly shake unsecured fittings lose. By the same token, wear can take place due to the continual movement at sea and on moorings and all moving parts and links in the rigging should be checked for this. This is a job for the annual refit when the whole rig can be stripped. Serious cruising and long passages will lead to wear, but this can be looked for, and often prevented with good layout.

Given careful design and maintenance there is no reason why a motorsailer should not sail well and reliably under most conditions. Sailing should be enjoyable for those who like the peace and quiet of using the wind, but also be efficient enough to be satisfying, and reliable to get safely to harbour in the event of engine failure. Most motorsailer rigs have a high safety margin built in to give reliability, and should be capable of reasonable windward performance. They have come a long way from the days when the sails were used only for steadying or when the wind was in the right direction: they are now sailing boats in their own right.

6 Sterngear

The underwater parts of a boat suffer greatly from neglect, probably on the basis that what you can't see you can ignore. The same applies to many cars: much more loving care is spent on polishing the outside than on cleaning and maintaining the engine, yet if the engine does not work, the clean exterior is not much use. When a boat is put into the water for a season's use the parts under water are not expected to require maintenance or attention, and it is much to the credit of designers and builders that these items do, in general, last out a season's use often in spite of considerable abuse.

The propeller and particularly the rudder are some of the most important parts of a boat: if anything goes wrong in this department there is little that can be done about it while at sea, and as far as the rudder is concerned there is usually no alternative available. Sails can push the boat along if the engine or propeller gives trouble, but steering is common to both these methods of propulsion and there is no real alternative. One could get a certain amount of steering from the sails or by rigging a jury rudder, but neither are easy to arrange or carry out.

Reliability of the rudder is paramount to the safe operation of a boat, and it can be achieved in two ways. Careful attention to design and construction will give a good basis, and from then on careful maintenance. The maintenance involved is minimal, and is mainly a question of checking that all is well or detecting wear long before it gets to serious proportions. Any change in the feel of the steering should be investigated straight away.

As with many things in the design of a motorsailer, its rudder has to perform well in two different modes. When sailing the rudder acts solely in the flow of water past the hull, but when motoring there is also an induced flow caused by the propeller slipstream, in which the rudder invariably lies. Fortunately these two conditions do not conflict to any large degree, and practical experience shows that the steering on most motorsailers can be pleasant under all conditions, given careful attention to design.

The first consideration in steering must be the hull shape, as it is this which has to be turned. Both the underwater and above-water shapes are involved, and where sails are carried, these as well. The effect of the wind on above-water forms and surfaces is very important when sailing, and in the last chapter the importance of balance between sails and hull was discussed at some length. The underwater shapes are equally important, particularly when under motor only.

It is mainly the profile or outline shape of the hull as seen from the side which affects its turning behaviour. The hull pivots about its centre of lateral resistance which is more or less at the geometric centre of the underwater profile. If the main underwater area is close to this point, i.e. if the keel is deep at the centre and the forefoot and stern are cut away, then the hull will turn easily and the steering will be light. On the other hand, if the underwater area is spread out along the length of the boat, say in a long straight keel, there will be much more resistance to turning. A deep forefoot is particularly detrimental to easy steering.

It is the underwater areas at the ends of the boat which largely affect the steering, as they exert a greater leverage about the centre of lateral resistance. The rudder should be hung well aft, where it will have the maximum steering effect. In general, underwater profiles of modern motorsailers show a cutaway forefoot terminating in a level keel extending for about a third of the length of the boat. The exceptions are in the motor-oriented examples where a longer straight keel is evident, but the powerful propeller thrust acting on the rudder (when motoring) compensates for any increased difficulty in turning the hull.

Not only does a hull have to turn easily when helm is applied, but it should also maintain a steady course when left to its own devices apart from the effect of external forces. Such directional stability is a requirement contradictory to easy turning. A long straight keel aids directional stability, and similarly keeping most of the underwater area aft. In the latter case the steering will be more affected by wind and waves. A boat can still be made to steer if an efficient rudder is fitted in conjunction with a long keel.

The steering effect of a rudder is proportional to speed through the water and approximately proportional to its area. 'Approximately' in the latter case as a rudder with a high aspect ratio, i.e. with a vertical depth considerably greater than its fore-and-aft length, is more efficient than a squarer shape. One of the problems with a motorsailer is that the rudder is required to be equally effective at high and low speeds when sailing and motoring. A compromise has to be reached so that the steering is not too heavy at full speed, but provides adequate control at slow speeds, with or without the effect of the propeller wash.

A rudder hung at its forward end will require a considerable effort to turn it. If its axis is moved slightly aft so that part of the blade is forward of it, less effort will be required to turn the rudder, which is influenced by the slipstream on both sides. This is known as a balanced rudder, due to the balancing effect of the area forward of the pivot or axis (6.1). This area should not exceed one-fifth of the area of the blade otherwise the rudder will become very tender and the steering will lose 'feel' and not self-centre. A

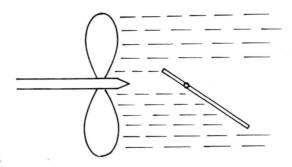

6.1

balanced rudder is particularly effective when working behind a large propeller as it will deflect more of the propeller thrust to one side than a rudder hung at the forward edge. This accounts for the good handling characteristics of many motorsailers when under power.

To provide the right degree of reliability the rudder and all its fittings must be adequately strong and of suitable materials. It is not an area where materials can be skimped for the sake of economy: this applies to the whole of the steering arrangements, and not just to motorsailers.

To actuate the rudder there are many differing systems available. The size of craft to which they are to be fitted will dictate the best type for the purpose, and those most commonly in use on motorsailers are the push–pull cable and the hydraulic. Where there is only one steering position the push–pull cable provides a relatively cheap, simple answer, with good reliability. This system gets complicated when two steering positions are required, and the changeover is not particularly simple. It is for this latter application that hydraulic systems come into their own, and also where routeing cables would be impossible. Such a system consists basically of a hydraulic pump at the wheel connected by pipes, either rigid or flexible, to a hydraulic ram at the rudder head. A secondary wheel is simply connected into the system, and either wheel can be used at any time without the other turning and without any changeover. It is more expensive, but it is simple to install, and reliable provided the basic maintenance required is carried out.

The best designed and constructed steering systems can still fail and all boats need to have some alternative means of moving the rudder. The simplest and most effective is to have the top of the rudder stock accessible either in a locker at the stern or via an access panel in the deck so that a tiller can be fitted. The usual system is to have a squared end on the rudder stock over which a squared socket on the tiller will fit. It may be hard work steering with a tiller, but it will get you home. The connection between the normal steering on the rudder stock should be easily disconnected so that it does not have to be turned as well. There has to be space for the emergency tiller to move, and for the helmsman.

For presumably sentimental reasons, the steering wheels on many boats still retain spokes on the outside. These do provide additional leverage when a small wheel has to be used, but the answer is to provide enough space for a larger wheel. It is rare to see a sailing boat's wheel these days with protruding spokes: the possibility of ropes and clothing fouling them is too well recognized. On motorsailers, the spoked wheel is retained in many cases where it is situated inside a wheelhouse. The danger from ropes fouling the wheel does not then occur, but the helmsman's clothing (or ribs) can get caught just as easily.

The gearing of the steering system is largely a matter for personal preference, but in general is somewhere between two and three turns from lock to lock when a large wheel is fitted. This gives enough feel for fine steering and the delicate adjustments required on passage without making manoeuvring in harbour too onerous. On larger boats where the increase in loading on the rudder can make hand steering difficult, some form of power assistance can be fitted. The most common is electro-hydraulic, which simply means that an electrically driven pump gives assistance in driving the hydraulic ram at the rudder stock. To take care of failure some form of manual over-ride is required. Some feel in the steering is lost with power assistance, and there is always the problem, when proceeding under sail alone, of the batteries being constantly drained unless some alternative means of charging is available.

Rudder failure is fortunately a fairly rare occurrence, and usually caused by neglect. If it occurs, one is fairly helpless unless a jury rudder can be rigged. It should be possible to steer a motorsailer on certain courses by balancing the sails; for instance, with the wind on the beam some form of steerage could be obtained by alternately slackening and hardening the jib. Try things out before they are required in earnest: if a rudder fails it is not likely to be in a flat calm but in a howling gale. Having some idea what to do can help a lot.

You may wonder at this dismal approach to what should be the pleasurable occupation of yachting, but on long open-water passages help may be a long way off. Apart from the hull itself, the rudder is the one essential component for which you do not have an obvious alternative. It behoves the prudent seaman to find one.

If the simple rudder has been made to appear complicated, then the propeller which drives the boat along when under power is an extremely complex piece of design which, as far as small boats are concerned, is not fully understood in theoretical terms. The propeller converts the power of the engine into forward motion of the boat, and in the final reckoning the efficiency of the propeller is a direct determinant of the efficiency of the boat under power. In ships, where a difference in speed of one-tenth of a knot can make a great deal of difference to the running efficiency, a great deal of research has been and still is being carried out on propeller design. On small craft (and especially pleasure craft) where the loss of a few horsepower is not the end of the world there is not the same demand for research and it lags behind that for big ships.

A great deal is known about propeller design for boats but there are so many variables involved that in the long run the experience of the propeller designer in assessing these is what counts. Hull shape will affect the design of a propeller, and unless a boat is to be built in large quantities there is neither the time nor the money available to carry out the exhaustive tests required to find the optimum propeller for that particular hull/power combination. In practice the variables are assessed largely in the light of experience with other boats of similar type and powering. To have propellers specially made for a particular application is expensive, and often the nearest approximation in a stock size is used. The resulting loss in efficiency should hardly be noticeable unless the selection is a long way out.

With motorsailers the position is even more complicated. When under power the most efficient propeller is required to transmit all of the engine power into forward thrust. When sailing, the propeller becomes just an appendage, producing drag and hindering the progress of the boat, and the larger the prop, the more drag. This is one more area in which the compromise between motoring and sailing can provide great difficulties for the designer, and much will depend on whether the final approach is to be motor or sailing oriented. In a motor-oriented design there will be little compromise in the design of the propeller, and its drag under sail will be accepted. The design of the propeller will then be limited only by the space for it to turn in and the power available.

The space available for the propeller will be determined by the hull design as it is usually unacceptable to have the propeller extending below the bottom of the keel. Such an arrangement is acceptable or even necessary on a planing boat, but on a motor-sailer which might be required to take the bottom, and will anyway be of greater draft, this is both undesirable and unnecessary. There is usually adequate room at the after end of the deadwood to swing a good-sized propeller without interfering with the lines of the stern, while still retaining an extension of the keel aft under the rudder to support the lower rudder bearing, and afford protection for the propeller and rudder (6.2).

If a propeller is to work efficiently it is important that there is adequate clearance between the tips of the blades and the surrounding hull. The minimum clearance should be in the order of one-sixth of the diameter of the propeller. Where it is working

6.2 A large, efficient propeller well below the waterline on this 36-footer. The hole in the balanced rudder allows the propeller shaft to be withdrawn without removing the rudder, and can be filled in with putty. The long keel and heel fitting both protect and support the rudder and propeller. (Banjer 36)

behind a deadwood, as is almost invariably the case on a single-screw motorsailer, there should also be a clearance of a similar amount between the deadwood and the leading edge of the propeller blades. These clearances give the propeller a chance to work in reasonably undisturbed water, although the water will always be disturbed to a degree by the flow round the hull.

For best results on yachts in the moderate speed range (which includes motorsailers) the propeller should have as large a diameter as is practicable. The clearances mentioned will be one limiting factor, but the speed of rotation will be another. The larger the propeller diameter, the slower it will turn for a given engine power, and the reduction gear necessary to reduce the engine speed will be selected accordingly. A common reduction usually available is about 3:1 which indicates the ratio of engine revolutions to shaft and propeller revolutions.

The pitch of a propeller determines the amount it can move forward with each revolution. Related to the propeller r.p.m. it gives an indication of the speed. A designer has some idea of the proposed speed in relation to engine power and r.p.m. and this gives him some idea of the pitch required on the propeller. The calculations are complicated by slip, which is the difference between the theoretical advance of the propeller for one revolution and that obtained in practice. It is a measure of the efficiency of the propeller, and good design will produce a slip of the order of 10 per cent.

To complicate the matter further, there is also a relationship between pitch and diameter for the best working. The pitch: diameter ratio is the critical figure here, and for motorsailers should be between 1 and 1.5, giving what is termed a nearly 'square' propeller, i.e. with pitch and diameter equal or nearly so.

When the basic size of the propeller has been decided the question of the number of blades to be used, their area and their shape all have to be considered. No wonder the propeller designer's job is complicated – but reasonably efficient propellers are produced.

On most motor-oriented motorsailers, a three-bladed propeller is chosen as giving the best compromise, transmitting power well and producing a minimum of vibration. Hull vibration (assuming proper alignment of engine, shafting and bearings) is mainly caused by the blanking-off of the propeller by the deadwood: with a three-bladed propeller only one blade at a time is blanked. However, by the same token, the two (or three) blades not blanked off when the propeller is fixed will intrude on the water flowing past the hull and cause drag when the boat is under sail. On sailing-oriented boats, where drag assumes a larger importance, a two-bladed propeller is sometimes fitted. This can be lined up behind the deadwood and the drag reduced. When motoring the blades will be alternately blanked and working fully, and this can cause unpleasant vibration, and wear. Careful fairing of the deadwood reduces such vibration, but will also increase drag as there is more flow around the propeller. On balance the three-bladed propeller is the usual choice and provides the best compromise. The effect of propeller drag is often over-estimated, and unless one is trying to get every last ounce of speed out of the boat the small reduction in speed is quite acceptable.

There is often much discussion about whether a propeller causes more drag when it is trailing, i.e. free to turn, or locked in one position. There is no doubt that it is better to have a two-bladed propeller locked out of the way behind the deadwood. With a three-bladed propeller there is also less drag when the shaft is locked; with the propeller free to turn, the friction of the shafting and the reduction gearing will add to the overall resistance. On boats fitted with a speedometer it is possible to detect a variation in speed when the shaft is locked, taking into account the normal variations of speed when sailing.

A propeller left to turn freely can cause problems apart from increased wear. The lubrication of most marine gearboxes is dependent on an oil pump which is driven from the input shaft of the gearbox. When the propeller and hence its shaft, and the output shaft of the gearbox to which it is solidly connected, are turning, the gearbox oil pump is not operating, which means that parts of the gearbox are turning without adequate lubrication. In the short term this is unlikely to cause any damage, but over a long period the bearings in the gearbox could be affected.

On most counts, then, it is desirable to lock the propeller shaft when the engine is not being used. There are many devices for this, ranging from simple clamps to sophisticated automatic devices. As with most things at sea, simplicity is the essence, but

6.3   A twin-screw 33 ft motorsailer. Note how exposed the propeller is, and how close to the waterline. The struts and long shafts will be a constant drag, in addition to the propeller itself. (Pelagian)

on the other hand any device fitted should either indicate its presence or free itself automatically when the engine is started. The most common devices are spring-loaded so that if the shaft is inadvertently put in gear with the brake on, it will allow the shaft to rotate, but make considerable noise in doing so, without causing damage. When a two-bladed propeller is fitted the shaft lock should fix the propeller in the vertical position to gain maximum benefit.

The propeller shaft is installed in an area where little work can be done at sea in the event of a problem, so it behoves the careful owner to give it attention when in harbour or each time the boat is slipped. Modern shafts are usually made of stainless steel or monel metal because of the corrosion dangers in this area. The size of the shaft will be governed by the engine horsepower, the size of propeller and the reduction gear; it should have a generous safety margin to allow for the excessive strains which might be imposed should the propeller become fouled. On most motorsailers the propeller is close to the deadwood so that there is no need for shaft brackets (6.3). The after bearing of the shaft is mounted either in or on the deadwood, with just a short length of shaft protruding; it will be either a metal-to-metal bearing or a rubber bearing. The former is lubricated by grease forced in from a greaser mounted conveniently inside the boat. A gland is fitted at the aft end to keep out sand and grit which would cause rapid wear. Rubber bearings are now commonly used but require a free flow of water to provide lubrication. When this type of bearing is mounted behind a deadwood, small scoops are provided on the bearing housing to divert water through the bearing. It ·is essential that these scoops are kept clear to maintain a good flow of water and every opportunity must be taken to clear them. They are a favourite spot for barnacles and other marine growth to congregate, particularly when a boat is left lying afloat and has not been used for a while; they also get painted over.

On a well regulated boat there should never be any possibility of ropes getting into the water and fouling the propeller. However it does happen, and if it is not ropes it will be plastic sheets or sacks which seem to be floating everywhere these days. If those ropes or plastic only foul the blades of the propeller one is lucky, and there is a good chance of getting them free, at least enough to use the engine. The real problem occurs when the rope or plastic finds its way into the gap between the propeller and the after shaft bearing housing. Here the friction set up will melt synthetic rope or plastic and at best it can only be removed by taking off the propeller. Until this can be done there is a distinct possibility that the engine will be unusable because of the excessive friction.

Because of this danger, the gap between the propeller boss and the bearing housing is made small and covered by a rope guard, which is simply a metal cover fastened to the bearing housing and extending over the propeller boss. When a rubber bearing is fitted care must be taken to maintain an adequate flow of water past the guard. Such a guard does not provide all the answers, but it can help.

At the inner end of the stern tube is the main gland, which

prevents water entering. This gland must be carefully packed and from time to time it will require adjustment. The greatest fear when adjusting this gland is of overtightening, which will cause the gland to run hot and could lead to eventual seizure. Although it is possible to adjust the stern gland so that it does not leak at all, in most cases a very slight leak is allowed as it indicates that provided all else is well, the gland has not been overtightened.

The bearing at this end of the stern tube is invariably a metal-to-metal bearing and again a greaser is fitted. These greasers should be worked before going to sea, and then about every eight hours. The usual location for the greasers is in the engine compartment, but I am sure they would be less likely to be overlooked if they were mounted more conspicuously and accessibly. If the shaft cannot be locked, this greaser must also be used regularly when sailing to keep the bearing lubricated.

Between the propeller shaft and the gearbox there may be two optional fittings. If a reduction gear is not integral within the gearbox then a separate reduction box may be fitted at the after end of the gearbox. This method makes varying the reduction ratio easier, but it adds one more oil level which has to be checked and is usually rather inaccessible. Its other advantage is to allow the engine and prop shafts to be offset from each other. The other fitting is a flexible coupling to allow the engine and shaft to move with a degree of independence. This is essential with a flexibly mounted engine, and desirable with a rigidly mounted one. In no way does the inclusion of a flexible coupling mean that engine and shaft do not have to be lined up properly, as the coupling can only work efficiently if this is done. You may wonder at the inclusion of a flexible coupling when both engine and shaft are rigidly mounted. The hull of a boat will flex to a certain extent, and the coupling will allow for these movements, but the biggest advantage is in its cushioning effect. Should the propeller strike something, the flexible coupling will reduce the strain on the gearbox and hopefully prevent any serious breakage.

The use of dissimilar metals in the sterngear introduce the problems of electrolytic corrosion. The rudder will often be of mild steel, the propeller of manganese bronze, and the propeller shaft of stainless steel. In sea water these have the makings of a good battery, with the mild steel suffering the most. To reduce the effect a zinc block is bolted to the rudder with careful electrical bonding so that it takes the brunt of the attack, leaving the remainder intact. The zinc will be slowly eaten away and will need replacing probably once a season.

For all that it is hidden away, the sterngear of any yacht contributes much to the performance and good handling. It will repay careful attention, but will not suffer neglect kindly. It bears repeating that a defect in this area will be very difficult if not impossible to rectify at sea, so time spent on maintenance is time well spent.

7 Accommodation

Designing the accommodation on yachts has developed into the art of fitting a quart into a pint pot. Over recent years there has been a dramatic increase in the accommodation space which can be fitted into a given overall length. This is not entirely due to clever interior design, although considerable ingenuity is shown in this respect. A study of old and modern designs will show that it is the hull shape which has changed. Hulls and superstructures are bulging and swelling in all directions, the main motive being to create more space down below. Hull size (in terms of length and volume), owners' needs, and superstructure all influence the design approach, and a variety of interior layouts are illustrated in this chapter.

Overall length is still a limiting factor in design, probably because most charges against a boat are based on its length. Length is thus an element of cost, but there is no such restriction on beam or height. Beam has increased in relation to length in recent years, and the current trend is to build upwards, with higher freeboards and cabin tops, so that the space down below is made more roomy. If this can be achieved without destroying the appearance of the boat, then something is gained.

Judging from advertisements, the measure of success in designing accommodation appears to be the number of berths which can be squeezed into a given length of boat. It is now quite normal to find six berths in a 30-footer. What has to be considered when looking at these berths is how many of them are usable at sea, and what space is left for the crew when they are not in their berths. There is also the question of stowing all of the personal belongings of this number of crew, as well as stores, warps, sails, fenders, etc.

The fact that designers go to great lengths to fit in as many berths as possible leads one to the conclusion that boats tend to be bought for use as houseboats or weekend cottages. Six berths in a small boat may be acceptable when alongside in a marina and the crew can step ashore to stretch their legs. Six people on board the same boat at sea in a moderate breeze can be absolute hell.

The concept of a motorsailer is comfortable and reliable cruising. Comfort on a long passage demands space to move about and space to stow one's belongings. All those on board should be able to be in the wheelhouse or cockpit at one time without being cramped, because this is where they will tend to congregate. Few people enjoy being below at sea unless they are sleeping or being forced to cook. A general rule for the numbers of crew for comfortable cruising would be one person for every 10 ft of length. This gives three on a 30-footer, which is adequate for both comfort and handling the boat. If this concept is borne in mind when choosing a boat, there will not be too much disappointment.

In trying to fit in as much accommodation as possible, designers have to resort to considerable ingenuity and adaptations to make interiors work. Some components have to perform dual roles, which often means that they have to be altered by the crew, e.g. tables which double as chart tables or bunk bottoms, or galley work surfaces which are also lids for sinks or storage space. This again is fine in harbour, but can prove difficult at sea. The need to alter and adapt in use should be kept to a minimum.

Sleep is important at all times, but particularly on passage when tiredness can lead to mistakes. A tired crew is a danger to both itself and others, and berths should be arranged to give as comfortable a sleep as is possible under the prevailing circumstances. It is to be said in favour of having plenty of berths in boat, that if the number of crew is kept down, at least they can pick the most comfortable of the berths for use at sea. If there is much motion it is necessary to secure one's body in the berth to prevent being thrown about, by means of leeboards.

Permanent leeboards which project above the level of the mattress and make an edge to the berth are out of fashion as they make the berths less comfortable as seats. Temporary boards or canvas mean that somewhere has to be found to stow them when not in use. The modern solution to the problem is the use of webbing straps extending from the outer edge of the berth to the deckhead or to the ship's side. These will stop you from falling out of the berth, but they will not prevent you rolling about, and you cannot jam your body in as you can with leeboards. If straps or leeboards are not used the solution appears to be to use all the berths on the lee side.

Taking home comforts to sea is now being carried as far as fitting double berths. These are a splendid idea when the boat is in harbour, allowing connubial bliss and saving space. At sea, however, a double berth is very impractical unless you are on extremely good terms with the person you are sharing the berth with. In any case the movement of the boat is almost sure to guarantee that neither of you get any sleep. The snag with the saloon double berth is that in the daytime it usually forms a dinette, so that before the berth can be used one has to wrestle with lowering the table and repositioning the cushions, not always an easy job when the boat is moving about. A place has to be found to stow the bedding in the daytime as well.

When studying the suitability of accommodation, the size of the berths has to be taken into account. In the effort to fit as many berths as possible into the minimum of space, it is not unknown for designers to take the odd inch or two off their length, which for anyone over 6 ft tall can make rest very uncomfortable. To fit most reasonably sized crew, a bunk should be 6 ft 6 in long with a width of 2 ft to 2 ft 6 in. Width is not so critical – in fact too wide a berth can make it difficult to wedge one's body within the space even when leeboards are fitted. Smaller berths are sometimes seen, advertised as 'children's berths', but not everyone has this requirement, and in the interests of standardization most are full size.

Apart from considerations of privacy and convenience, the position of berths is not very important when in harbour. At sea, berths in the bow and stern can be subject to a lot of movement when the boat is pitching or pounding, which can make them

uncomfortable to the point of being unusable. When sailing to windward, berths right forward are subjected to large vertical movements which can cause one to alternately levitate and then try to disappear through the mattress. This is not conducive to a good night's sleep.

I have gone on at some length about sleeping arrangements to demonstrate how some yachts fall short when it comes to practicality and comfort at sea. A boat is bought after an inspection in harbour, and at best a short trial sail. A night at sea would provide a much better test and would make the prospective purchaser aware of more shortcomings. Many of the snags in the accommodation can be overcome by simple modification, but the main point to remember is that a boat which boasts of having six berths does not necessarily have this number fit or available for use at sea.

The interior design of boats now owes a lot to caravans (house trailers) in the ingenuity shown in providing home facilities within a confined space. Here the similarity ends, as the interior of a boat has to be built to much higher standards to withstand the stresses which can be placed on it. These stresses are caused not only by the movement of the boat itself, but by the sometimes violent movement of the crew within the boat. A crew member who loses his balance within the cabin because of an unexpected movement will grab at the first thing that comes to hand. All fittings liable to be attacked in this way should be strong enough to prevent damage to the fitting and injury to the crew. Handholds should be provided in all areas and these must be well constructed and fastened.

There was a time when labour was cheap and good timber

7.1 A fibreglass motorsailer near the top of the size range for production boats, and one of a series from the same builder. Ketch rig is seen almost without exception on motorsailers of this size, as well as ample walk-through accommodation and large cockpits. From amidships aft the sections decrease in beam far less than on a cruiser, so there is relatively little tapering of the hull towards the transom. Performance under power can benefit; the other advantage of course is in increased accommodation, stowage, tankage and engineroom space. Although there is ample overall length and freeboard, a continuous coachroof is employed to open out the accommodation. (Gulfstar 53 M S)

obtainable at a reasonable price. The interiors of boats would be hand built of selected wood and a matter of pride for both builder and owner. For the mass-produced motorsailer today such an approach is no longer practical or economical, and large parts of the interiors are now constructed from fibreglass mouldings. While these form the basis of the construction, tradition still dies hard, and much better quality timber is still used to disguise and trim the somewhat cold mouldings.

Mouldings for the interior construction can make cleaning and maintenance much easier but they do reduce the possibilities of modifying the interior to suit individual preference. The amount of modification which a builder is prepared to undertake will depend largely on his commitment to mass-production methods and on the number of boats of that type which he is building. It will always cost extra to vary a standard layout, but generally speaking the standard specifications on motorsailers are to a fairly high standard. Alteration is also restricted where interior mouldings also act as hull stiffening, which is often the case.

Apart from the sleeping berths, which take up a lot of the usable space, room has to be found for cooking facilities, toilet area, stowage for the many items of loose equipment and somewhere to eat. If there is not space in the wheelhouse, room also has to be found to store and spread out charts and do the navigating. Headroom is an important consideration in some of these areas, particularly in the galley and toilet area, if contortions are to be avoided. Full headroom usually means about 6 ft 3 in, which should be provided in the main areas of movement. It is often restricted to the centre of the boat where the depth of the cabin sole and the height of the coachroof make it possible, but headroom is now a far stronger priority than it once was.

Cooking facilities on all cruising yachts have long changed from the time when a single-burner alcohol or kerosene (paraffin) stove was considered adequate. People now demand all the comforts of home when they go to sea and this commonly extends to the provision of a stove, oven and refrigerator; running water is taken for granted. If all these facilities are to be fitted into a boat, and still leave room for other things, careful planning of the galley is required. Anyone brave enough to prepare meals at sea deserves special consideration, and the best possible facilities to make the job as easy, quick and pleasant as possible. Meals at sea on a long passage are important from a morale point of view, but are difficult to produce if the boat is tossing about. So often one sees the cook producing a splendid meal and then being unable to eat because he or she has been shut up down below for too long preparing it.

The motorsailer can offer several advantages here. If the galley is sited below, at least it can be placed close to the companionway which will give the cook some communication with the outside world. Unless conditions are very bad, the wheelhouse or shelter will in most cases offer sufficient protection so that the access doors can be left open. Unless there is a galley extractor fan cooking smells will invade the wheelhouse, but if the cook has to suffer them, why shouldn't everyone else? Another disadvantage is that steam from the cooking may mist up the windows, reducing visibility, but adequate ventilation in the wheelhouse should cure this.

Where a large enclosed wheelhouse exists it is possible to install the galley in the wheelhouse. This trend is becoming apparent on some motor cruisers and there is no reason why it should not extend to motorsailers. The advantages are many, both at sea and in harbour, but it does raise some problems not least of which is the use of valuable space in the wheelhouse which many owners, acting the part of Captain, will look on as their personal domain.

One can sense reaction against having the galley in the wheel-house from the fact that it seems rather like taking your visitors on board through the kitchen door. Perhaps the answer lies in a com-promise, by keeping the main galley down below but having a small (perhaps single-burner) stove in the wheelhouse for use when conditions are bad or when people are sleeping down below. One of the snags of having any type of burner in the wheelhouse is that the flame will be affected by drafts when windows or doors are open for ventilation. An alternative is to use an electric kettle, as in many cases a hot drink is all that is required. Kettles do place a very heavy drain on batteries, but with modern alternator charging this should not be too excessive if the correct type of kettle is chosen. It should only be used when the engine is running, but it will enable water to be boiled even when the boat is moving about quite violently.

The key point of any galley is the stove, and those suitable for the production motorsailer come in three types, varying in the fuel used. Butane or propane gas is the easiest to use, but stoves of this type are not allowed to be installed below decks in some countries. There is a risk attached if the gas should leak: it is heavier than air and will sink into the bilges; mixed with air it can form an explosive mixture which can be detonated by a spark or possibly a hot part of the engine. Detectors are available which will indicate the presence of the gas in the bilges, which must then be well ventilated before anything electrical is used or a match is struck. Gas cylinders should be stowed in separate compartments draining overboard or on deck so that any leakage will not collect in the bilges. They should be turned off when the stove is not in use, and the piping carefully installed and checked for leaks at frequent intervals.

Modern kerosene (paraffin) stoves are easier to use and more odourless than their predecessors, but there is still a delay in getting them started. This is not too inconvenient in harbour but can prove a nuisance at sea. The fuel is cheap and readily obtainable, and the main danger is of a flare-up. A disadvantage is that

---

7.2 The interior layout of this 46-footer includes some power cruiser features which would not be expected on conventional sailing auxiliaries. The division of living/sleeping quarters into three areas separated by two head and stowage compartments is now seen on many cruising boats, and usually implies family use or two or three couples sailing together. However, this amount of engine space and provision for tools, spares and workbench is rarely seen except on power craft, or those motorsailers where the power aspect is more than an afterthought and has been allotted a realistic share of available space. This encourages good accessibility and installation, and a higher standard of maintenance and repairs later on. The main saloon is partially above deck level, under a high coachroof and enclosed by nine large windows: underway the choice lies between an open cockpit or a totally sheltered living area with excellent visibility (similar to (3.3) and in contrast to (7.3)). The galley and chart table are at the forward end of this area; alternatively, the dinette can be replaced by a 9 ft L-shaped settee and the chart table moved amidships under the cockpit. The galley occupies a major part of the saloon, and is very well equipped with icebox (or refrigeration), hot and cold pressure water system, salt water pump, stove and lockers. Externally, these elements in the design are not heavily emphasized, and the overall profile is that of a long-keeled cruiser with an effective sail area. (Cal 2-46)

Accommodation

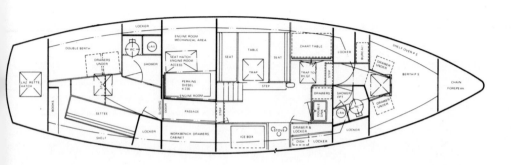

there is no built-in grill or oven. Attachments can be obtained which sit on top of the burner but these are not very practical at sea. Kerosene stoves are very safe if kept clean and maintained regularly, but the delay in starting them up does demand that cooking is planned carefully, and inhibits fixing a quick hot drink.

The alcohol stove is rapidly gaining favour on cruising boats, particularly in those countries where bottled gas stoves are not allowed. It lacks the instant starting of gas, but it is much easier than kerosene. The fuel is not yet readily obtainable in some areas and is comparatively expensive, but it burns with a hot clean flame and is not explosive. Grills and ovens can be used and the appearance of the stove is very similar to the gas types.

Whatever type of stove is chosen, regular maintenance and cleaning will be required to ensure trouble-free operation. It is arguable whether stoves should be gimballed or fixed, but with the larger units now being used gimballing is not easy to engineer. The oven and grill are rarely used at sea, and if good fiddles are fitted to the top burners to stop pans sliding about, this should be adequate for most purposes. Fiddles can be fitted to the oven as well.

A sink with hot and cold running water is now considered as normal in many motorsailers, but adds considerable complication to the plumbing system. Water pressure is maintained by an electric pump which switches on automatically when the tap is turned on. This is fine while the pump is working, but if it fails or the batteries are flat it is as well to have some alternative means of getting water out of the tanks. It would be very frustrating to have gallons of fresh water on board and no means to get at it. A small hand-operated pump is fitted on some boats for this purpose, and to discourage over-consumption.

Hot water can be provided by two methods. Bottled gas used for cooking can also fuel a small water heater which lights automatically when the hot tap is turned on, heating only the water needed. These are similar to some domestic gas water heaters, and if one accepts the risks associated with using gas, they are very satisfactory. Kerosene and alcohol could be used for water heating but they would not work automatically, and it would be just as easy to heat the water on the stove. The alternative is to use the waste heat from the engine in a calorifier. Hot water from the engine cooling system is passed through pipes in an insulated tank connected to the domestic fresh water system. By heat exchange the tank water is heated and is available at the hot tap. Disadvantages of this system are that the engine has to run to heat the water, and the water will gradually cool as the hot water is used up. However it is a cheap system to install, uses no fuel directly, and is absolutely safe.

On a well equipped yacht the galley equipment is completed by a refrigerator. Provision is made for installation on most motor-sailers if they are not fitted as standard equipment. They can be run off bottled gas or electricity, the latter being generally favoured from the safety angle. The electric refrigerator does make demands on the battery when the engine is stopped, unless switched off, but otherwise works as efficiently as its domestic counterpart. Refrigeration can also be provided by equipment run directly off the engine by belt drive. The alternative to a refrigerator is an icebox; however ice is not always readily obtainable or of practical size, particularly when cruising, and the advent of the small refrigerator is slowly killing off the icebox.

Storage space for pots, pans, crockery, cutlery and food has to be found in the galley area. Not only must the stowage be secure to prevent these items from being thrown about, but they should also be readily available and convenient. Deep, large lockers where one has to search through layers of tins or pots are maddening. Apart from the need to secure pots on the top of the stove with fiddles, there is also the need to secure things on the work tops, and cups, plates etc when preparing a meal.

A fully equipped galley can place considerable demands on the space within the hull. Much ingenuity is shown in designing compact galleys and the result gives the cook little excuse for not preparing decent meals. The complication of the modern galley is fully justified on cruising boats, but for weekend use one wonders. However, few owners are likely to quibble if they want to get their wives or girlfriends to do the cooking.

The hot water supply to the galley is usually piped to the toilet compartment as well so that the convenience of hot and cold running water is available. This is another area where home comforts are demanded. To fit a toilet, wash basin and shower into a space less than 3 ft square demands considerable ingenuity; on some boats it also requires considerable contortion to use them, such is the restriction of space. The fitting of showers in even quite small boats is a welcome feature, and enables one to freshen up after a long passage at sea. In the limited space available in the head it is inevitable that everything gets wet when the shower is used, and the compartment has to be suitably lined and drained to cope with this. Any stowage for toilet articles, towels etc has to be planned with this in mind, or placed elsewhere. Regular cleaning is essential if the compartment is not to start smelling.

Both the wash basin and toilet can discharge overboard if pollution laws allow. The drain for the shower will be in the floor and below the waterline so that it cannot drain straight overboard. In some areas it is not permissible to let waste drain overboard, particularly in harbour, and many motorsailers are now being fitted with waste holding tanks. Everything drains into this tank which is fitted with either a hand or electric pump for emptying at sea or pumping out ashore as the situation permits. Where such a tank is not fitted, the shower drain usually runs into the bilge and is then pumped overboard. Unless strict cleanliness is observed, and the bilge cleaned regularly, this is likely to lead to nasty smells eventually, and foreign matter in the bilges which can clog pumps.

WCs or toilets come in various types and what is fitted will depend largely on what space and local practice allow. There is strong feeling about allowing raw sewage to be discharged straight overboard, and electrical and chemical toilets are becoming more common. The electric type recycles the purified sewage, but both types have to be emptied at intervals which can be an unpleasant chore. Many marinas and docks now provide good sewage facilities, which is helping to overcome this problem.

Both the toilet compartment and the galley are areas which require particular attention to ventilation. This is a somewhat neglected area of boat design, and what is done is on a piecemeal basis, fitting a ventilator where it is thought some ventilation is required. Good ventilation can add greatly to the pleasure of life on board both in harbour and at sea, and it can also help to preserve any boat. This may seem irrelevant with fibreglass boats where there is nothing to rot; however, much of the cabin is supported on timber bearers and framing and rot starting here can be difficult to cure. Much of the timber used in this area is only of moderate quality and thus more prone to rot. Linings and upholstery can become mildewed and decay from dampness. Ventilation should operate when battened down in heavy weather or when the boat is left unattended at its moorings. When living on board in harbour ventilation is easy to achieve because hatches and windows can be opened, but even then the bilges and other semi-enclosed areas only get ventilated by accident rather than by design.

There are two main sources of damp in a boat. One is from condensation on the cold sides and deck, and the other from water which finds its way below on wet clothing or through minor leaks. Condensation comes from water vapour in the air, which can condense from the waste gases from burners, heaters, from steam from cooking, and from the human body. Showers also add their quota. When battened down, condensation can be a considerable nuisance unless there is good ventilation, and yet there appears to be little constructive effort to achieve this.

The object of a ventilating system is to get a through draft of air below decks, introducing fresh air and expelling the contaminated, moist air. For a system to work in bad weather it is undesirable to have an entry point for fresh air forward, so some form of return system has to be devised. The space between the cabin sole and the tank tops can provide a return channel. As this area should be ventilated anyway, it serves a dual purpose. The flow of fresh air should then be from aft, and inevitably via the wheelhouse, flowing forward through the accommodation to a point where it can enter the bilges and flow aft again. All very nice in theory, but air will not flow in such a manner unless blown or sucked. The amount of air required to be moved is not large, but to rely on natural forces is a bit hit-and-miss, particularly in view of the somewhat devious and constricted channels involved.

The engine requires a great deal of air in running and this is normally drawn from the engine compartment, which is fitted with ventilators to the outside. If the engine air intake were diverted via the cabin bilge it would still receive its required quantity of air (assuming the bilges were not sealed), and at the same time induce a flow of air around the cabin. To ensure that the engine's air supply was not cut off accidentally, a good-sized air inlet that can be left open in all weathers would have to be fitted to the cabin. The devious passage of air to the engine may result in a slight falling-off in performance, but with the adequate power available

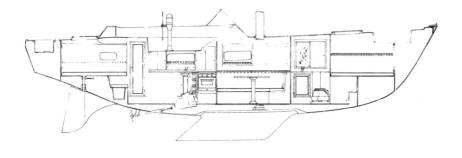

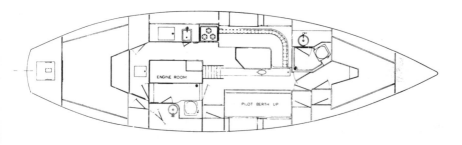

7.3 Layout within a raised cockpit, flush-decked hull. The three-section division (3.1, 7.1, 7.2) is utilized, but the galley is next to the engine compartment rather than in the main saloon, with the after cabin's head on the other side. Large ports in the topsides provide illumination and alleviate any closed-in effect in the after cabin, saloon and galley/head areas; Lucite deck hatches serve the same purpose. There is no superstructure apart from the high cockpit sides and spray screen, and the topsides are correspondingly raised in order to contain the accommodation and give full walk-through headroom. A large proportion of the fin and skeg hull is out of water for this reason, and also to reduce wetted surface. (Coronado 41)

on most motorsailers this should not be significant. With thought, it is often possible to facilitate air flow through cabin joinery, lockers or ducts.

This system of ventilation would be fine while the engine was running, and for periods when it was not an electric fan could be introduced into the system, or alternatively a good natural extractor vent. The latter will work well if it is carefully selected and installed, but must be capable of easy and totally secure closure in bad weather otherwise it will allow water in rather than take air out. Any system of ventilation should allow air both to enter and leave the enclosed space, so usually two ventilators are needed. If they also draw air from the bilges this will hopefully maintain rather than counteract the desired circulation pattern.

Any comprehensive ventilation system will require a certain amount of trial and error to get right, and the resulting ducting may turn out a little complicated. Smoke can be used to detect the air flow, and if done properly the resulting improvement in the accommodation will be well worthwhile, and better than some of the haphazard systems now used.

Introducing fresh air into the accommodation is fine when the weather is warm as it will help to make the interior cool and pleasant. However, a motorsailer is meant for possible use all the year round, and in cold weather a steady draft of fresh air will not be very welcome. The flow of air can be stopped (with a build-up of humidity and probably fumes and odours), but in many cases some form of heating is also required. Boat heaters are of various types, and are being fitted as standard equipment on some motorsailers.

One of the simplest is really an extension of the water heating system which works by heat exchange off the engine. The heated cooling water is lead through a radiator over which a fan blows air, the warmed air being directed as required. This suffers from the same disadvantage as the engine water heater in that the engine has to be running to get any heat: in harbour, where heating is most often required, there would be none. Other systems use diesel oil, kerosene (paraffin), butane or propane gas, and it may be logical to use the same fuel as the engine to obviate the need for extra tanks. This explains the popularity of the small diesel fuelled heaters frequently found on motorsailers and motor cruisers. They do require a small amount of electrical power to drive the fan and for starting, but the drain on the batteries is small and within the capabilities of most systems.

Kerosene heaters are similar to diesel units except for the different fuel used. Both use ducted hot air to heat the accommodation and the combustion fumes from the heater are led to a small outlet in the coachroof. In some cases this outlet incorporates the air inlet as well so that the installation is very compact. Other systems rely on drawing air from the compartment in which the heater is mounted, so this must be well ventilated; again, in harmony with the normal circulation pattern. Because both systems circulate warm fresh air they virtually eliminate condensation in the cabin and serve to both heat and ventilate.

Diesel heaters are usually mounted in the engine compartment to keep the fuel system compact and so that the noise of the heater does not intrude. Kerosene heaters with their separate fuel requirements can be mounted in any convenient space, but are often in the main cabin.

If bottled gas is used for cooking and water heating then it may be convenient to use it for cabin heating also. Heaters can be either of the standard gas fire type (which can be dangerous because of the naked flame) or of the catalytic type which is more like a radiator in appearance. The latter are common on boats because of their greater safety, but like all gas appliances both types do produce fumes and water vapour when working. If gas is to be used for cooking, water heating and cabin heating, then very careful attention will have to be paid to the ventilation of the cabin spaces.

One further method of heating is with a coal or coke stove. It is messy, requires a lot of attention, takes up a lot of space, can be dangerous and the fuel is difficult to stow, yet there is nothing quite so pleasant on a cold evening. Solid fuel stoves are definitely for the enthusiast, but although they raise many problems, they can give an air of pleasure and comfort quite unlike anything else. Fumes and hot components are the source of danger: the fuel itself has the virtue of being quite harmless.

In the sometimes doubtful efforts to make maximum use of space within hulls there have been many interesting design innovations. The standard layout of two-berth cabin forward and a main saloon amidships is still found in most motorsailers. There is a trend

Accommodation

7.4A

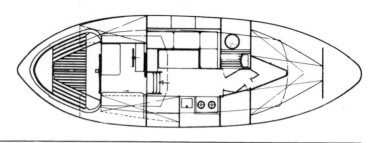

7.4B

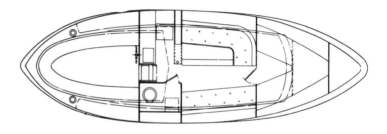

7.4C

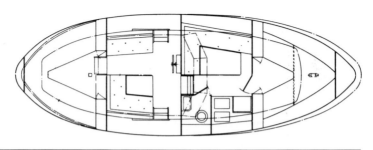

7.4D

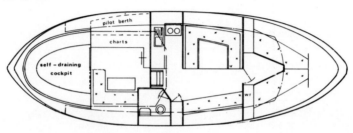

Accommodation

7.4E

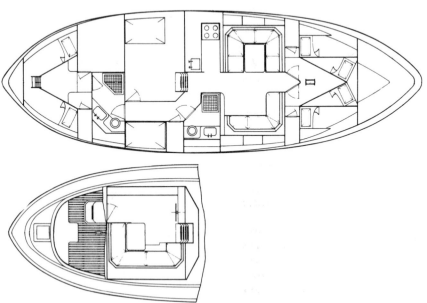

towards incorporating the saloon with the wheelhouse in some designs, so that in effect they become one large compartment on two levels (7.4). This gives a greater feeling of spaciousness down below and does keep the cook in touch with what is going on outside, and in easy reach of fresh air. The traditional location for the toilet is between the forward and main compartments so that it can serve either and still retain privacy, but against this is that anyone sleeping in either cabin is often disturbed when the toilet is used. The same argument holds good for the navigating area when this is in the saloon, and there is no one layout which will satisfy all requirements. It is only on the larger sizes of yachts that the accommodation can be designed to give privacy where required and separate the various functions.

One method adopted on smaller boats to break up the accommodation and give greater flexibility is to incorporate an after cabin. This provides two berths in a self-contained space, albeit with little room for anything else in the smaller boats. In large

---

7.4 Five related motorsailers from the same builder which illustrate possible variations in layout, superstructure and image, and the connection between interior layout, superstructure and size. (A) and (B) have identical fibreglass hull mouldings, displacements and sailplans; (C) has a slightly different hull with 10 in greater beam but otherwise the same dimensions, displacement, sailplan and engine. However, (A) has a characteristic 'heavy weather' or 'trawler' look with raked wheelhouse lines recalling fishing craft, an enclosed steering position and short deep cockpit; (B) has a very different 'lid' or upper moulding, giving a more open steering position and larger cockpit, and visually a quite different effect. (C) is clearly from the same stable, but has a larger enclosed wheelhouse with an after cabin replacing the cockpit, and a conventional motorsailer profile. In terms of accommodation, (A) and (C) have some of the sleeping and sitting spaces in the wheelhouses, whereas (B), which is more an 'outdoors' scheme, has the service areas of galley and head just forward of the cockpit and the living spaces all within the hull. Having greater length and beam but very similar proportions, (D) can combine these elements so that a cockpit, wheelhouse with accommodation inside, and the same number of below-decks berths and service areas are all fitted in; on (E), which is larger still, an after cabin, second head, larger engineroom, linking passageway below the wheelhouse, and more saloon and forward cabin space are added. (Fisher 30, Caribbean 30, Northeaster 30, Fisher 37, Fisher 46)

motorsailers the after cabin can provide very acceptable accommodation, particularly when access can be from the main accommodation without going on deck. The extra privacy afforded is welcome, and it can give an owner the chance to escape from his guests or charterers (and vice versa). In a smaller motorsailer the desirability of an after cabin must be carefully considered as other useful features may have to be sacrificed. The after cockpit will be the first thing to go, and to many people this will not be acceptable. To the owner who likes to sail the aft cockpit may be too much of a sacrifice, which probably explains why such cabins are more usually found on the motor-oriented type of motorsailers (7.4). A cockpit is still possible, but it will have to be placed more amidships and is often combined with a shelter (3.1) or raised and open (3.2) rather than a full wheelhouse. Where a wheelhouse exists, the idea of a cockpit is usually abandoned altogether. Access to the interior is from inside the wheelhouse and the boat becomes totally enclosed.

An after cabin may be very attractive at a boat show, but on a hull under 35 ft in length the whole arrangement both above and below deck can be very cramped by trying to fit it in. Deck space is reduced, the boat can appear cramped up, cockpit space is reduced, and it is likely to be noisy with the propeller shaft underneath. Clever design can improve many of these factors, but the only real gain in having an after cabin is in the privacy it offers. It can give parents a chance to escape from their children, which can be important on a small boat, and it can offer an undisturbed sleep at sea away from the rest of the crew using the galley and toilet forward. Access presents one of the main drawbacks of the after cabin arrangement (3.1). For convenience the hatch is usually at the forward end, giving access from the cockpit but open to all the water and spray flying about. An access in the after end of the cabin means a clamber around the (usually narrow) deck to get below. The after cabin only really succeeds where there is a fully enclosed wheelhouse and its access is protected inside, or where it is only from below.

Dividing up space below with bulkheads can increase the cramped look of the accommodation, but bulkheads are necessary to give privacy and in most cases strength to the hull. Modern fibreglass boats need little in the way of full bulkheads to add to the strength of the hull except in way of the mast, and this often accounts for the placing of the toilet compartment and hanging lockers at this point. A bulkhead in the bow can be a useful safety feature in the event of collision, but to be effective it must be strong as it will have to withstand considerable pressure, and should extend well below the waterline. The space thus enclosed usually contains the chain locker. Engine compartment bulkheads should be watertight to prevent oil, water, fumes and noise from entering the accommodation, and to keep water out of the engine area. This provides a safety factor in the event of hull damage to either space, but making bulkheads watertight is not always easy in view of the pipes and wires which have to pass through them.

Accepting that the space below has to be divided up to a certain extent, much can be done by means of the internal decoration to create an effect of spaciousness. Horizontal lines across a bulkhead will make a cabin seem wider, and light colours will create space. Such horizontals can be formed by the careful placing of shelves, handholds etc. It also helps to make the full width of the cabin visually apparent; it should be possible to see the sides of the hull on both sides to get the impression of its full width. So often they are filled up with lockers to obtain the maximum stowage. There is much that an experienced interior designer can do to improve yachts, and such specialized services are being used more often.

Stowage space for personal gear and boat equipment is always a problem, and there never seems to be enough: one is not necessarily expected to look scruffy on small boats. Reasonably smart clothes require suitable stowage. Equipment is usually stowed in lockers around the cockpit, and if these are large enough they can often hold sails as well. Otherwise sail stowage is usually one (or more) of the berths. Another drawback of an after cabin is that it can considerably reduce the deck or cockpit stowage space.

On a motorsailer there is plenty of scope for creating a homely and comfortable atmosphere which can be equally suitable for passing quiet hours in harbour or rough nights at sea. The owner is the only person who can add the individual touches which can give a boat its own character. The accommodation is the main area where this can be done on the mass-produced boats of today, particularly as this is one area where some builders will still make modifications to owners' requirements.

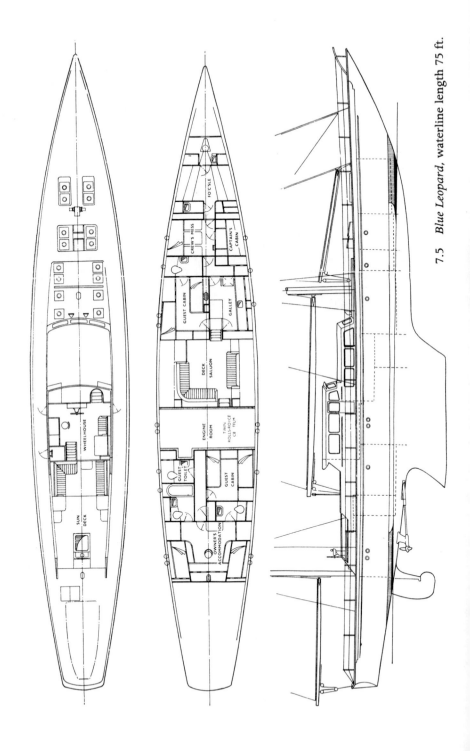

7.5 *Blue Leopard*, waterline length 75 ft.

SUN
DECK

WHEELHOUSE

FO'C'SLE

CREW'S MESS

CAPTAIN'S
CABIN

GUEST CABIN

GALLEY

DECK
SALOON

ENGINE
ROOM

TWIN
ROLLS-ROYCE
C8 TECM

GUEST
TOILET

GUEST
CABIN

OWNER'S
ACCOMMODATION

8 Equipment

Builders of yachts have two approaches to equipping their craft. They can provide a more or less comprehensive inventory so that the owner can step on board and go off to sea. This is fine provided the builders can anticipate accurately what the prospective owner requires and wants, but owners tend to be individuals who have their own ideas and anticipation is difficult. As well as preference it is also a question of price, some people being in the position where they can afford a host of equipment whereas others make do with the necessities, or transfer equipment from other boats they have owned. The course most builders adopt is to provide a boat with basic requirements and then offer a long list of optional extras. The basic equipment is often that which can only be fitted during construction because of the work involved, but more often is just sufficient for the boat to sail and motor so that it can be demonstrated. Here the argument is that personal preference in equipment can best be met by allowing the customer to specify his requirements. Where the equipment thus specified has to be incorporated at the building stage, careful thought is required.

Frequently motorsailers are sold in many countries other than the builder's, causing difficulty in meeting particular local statutory requirements or recommendations from a standard inventory. This is another reason for leaving the choice to the prospective owner, or perhaps to some degree to the selling agent in the country concerned. Equipment of foreign manufacture may be difficult to get service and spares for; likewise a handbook in a language other than that of the country of manufacture. This is becoming less of a problem, but a prospective owner should consider this point, particularly with regard to more complex equipment and machinery.

Safety equipment and safe installations is one area where countries differ in their requirements, whether these exist as mandatory rules or recommended standards. Insurers increasingly also have their say, and sometimes insist on certain standards, particularly in respect of fire-fighting equipment and inflammable fuels.

Fire at sea can be frightening in view of the lack of assistance available: it is fortunately not frequent. The causes stem from two main sources, the galley and the engine; there is also the risk of electrical fires from short circuits and the usual one from smoking. Little attention appears to be paid to fireproofing boats, so once a fire has got a hold it could develop rapidly, especially in fibreglass. The equipment provided must thus be directed to both detecting fire at an early stage and extinguishing it.

In the accommodation a fire is reasonably likely to be detected quickly in the absence of detection equipment, but it is in the engine compartment that it is most likely and also hardest to detect until it has got a good hold. In a motorsailer, with the helmsman invariably standing on top of the engine compartment, a fire can burn for a considerable time without detection. Even then the first sign is likely to be a reduction in the engine revolutions as the fire starves it of air, or smoke is sucked into the air intake. When this happens, the immediate reaction is to lift the engine hatches to find out what is wrong, allowing more air to get to the fire.

Various systems are available to both give warning of a fire in the engine compartment and extinguish it. The simplest system doesn't give a warning, but has a heat plug which allows an extinguishing gas to escape when the temperature reaches a pre-set level. These are good and reliable, and meet the needs of most motorsailer installations. More sophisticated types have a warning light or alarm fitted at the instrument panel which lights up when the temperature in the engine compartment reaches a predetermined level, and it is then up to the helmsman to actuate the built-in extinguisher(s). With this latter system, the helmsman has a better idea of what is going on, and the option of activating extinguishers.

Other types of fire on board can best be dealt with by portable extinguishers, but these must be of a type suitable for the situation. Electrical *fires* (not explosions set off by sparks etc) do not normally present the same hazard as in a home because of the low voltages involved. The exception is in the case of radio or radar equipment. Extinguisher size must be adequate for prolonged use: the little pint-sized extinguishers are virtually useless for all but the smallest of fires. Do not necessarily go for the largest and heaviest as they will be found very difficult to use in a seaway. Dry powder extinguishers are virtually useless at sea as the powder settles and becomes compacted with the movement of the boat. Propellants and extinguishing substances are subject to regulation or bans in some countries.

Fire fighting is an important consideration on small boats and is an area where builders could do more to impose a good standard. On nearly all of the new motorsailers I have seen, provision has been limited to the fitting of one or at best two extinguishers, which is hardly sufficient. In a boat surrounded by water it is possible to make use of this unlimited medium for extinguishing purposes, given adequate connections on the bilge pumps, be they engine, electric or hand driven, so that water can be sucked in via a seacock and discharged through a hose. The connections and valves are simple, and such a hose could serve as a deck wash as well, although in these days of contaminated sea water and fibre-glass decks there is not the same requirement for this as previously.

The other safety equipment required is intended for attracting attention if help is needed, and to abandoning ship if it is not forthcoming. In the former category are included hand flares, parachute flares and smoke flares. Recommendations or regulations as to numbers and types vary considerably from country to country and with the use to which the boat is to be put. For a motorsailer with its clear capability for offshore cruising, a minimum of six parachute flares should be carried; they can be supplemented by hand and smoke flares but the parachute flare is the only one which can be seen for any considerable distance. At night and in good visibility, this could be up to ten miles. Hand flares are suitable when close inshore or a rescuer is near, but their range is limited.

Similarly with smoke flares, the range is limited and on a windy day the smoke disperses very quickly indeed. When you use a distress flare you usually need help badly, hence the emphasis on the parachute flare – far and away the most effective and, as usual, also the most expensive. All flares should be stowed where they are ready to hand but also where they will always stay dry. On a motorsailer this invariably means in the wheelhouse. The stowage should be such that the flares cannot roll around otherwise there is always the chance of them going off prematurely or not working when required. Finally, always respect the expiry date stamped on the flares. It goes against the grain to throw away what appears to be a perfectly good flare, but if you want them to work when you really need them, it is the only way. Or at least *replace* the outdated flares, even if you decide to keep the older ones just in case.

Included in the category of equipment for abandoning ship are liferafts, lifejackets and lifebuoys. The average motorsailer is basically a sound and seaworthy boat, but the unexpected does happen and even the best run boat can get into trouble by, say, hitting a floating object at night. With the extended cruising capability of the motorsailer such an event could happen a long way from land and help, and a liferaft could save the day. They are expensive pieces of equipment, however, and each owner will have to decide whether the cost is justified. In some countries he has no choice as a liferaft is mandatory, but otherwise the decision will be governed by the use to which the yacht is put. For near coastal work and sheltered waters it will probably be adequate if a dinghy is carried, the assumption being that help is always near at hand. By performing two functions the dinghy earns its keep. Offshore, I would consider a liferaft essential, and in winter under any conditions it is again essential. The shelter and warmth provided by the liferaft canopy are very necessary in these conditions, and a dinghy cannot provide them.

Suitable stowage for a liferaft (for most motorsailers, at least a six-man raft) is difficult to arrange. Space below is usually too restricted, and anyway the raft should be on deck where it can be rapidly launched. It usually ends up on the foredeck where there is most space, but here it is exposed to seas coming on board, and unless securely lashed is liable to come adrift in heavy weather. Secure lashings may hinder easy launching, so that on balance the best place is on deck but aft, if space can be found. The end of the raft's painter must be made fast and the lashings fitted with quick-release hooks. The weight of a liferaft is considerable, so remember when choosing a stowage that the raft may have to be manhandled over the side in heavy weather (or up out of the cockpit). A conveniently placed gap or opening section in the lifelines can be very helpful here. Fibreglass containers for liferafts offer very good protection against the elements and against chafe due to movement, but are slippery and hard to hold onto or lash down, compared to a valise. Getting up such a case from stowage below decks can be surprisingly difficult.

Lifejackets are logically the ultimate defence one has against the sea, keeping you afloat for a long time to give your rescuers a chance of finding you. In cold water the limiting factor on survival is not keeping afloat, but exposure: cold water can render you unconscious in a matter of minutes rather than hours. A good life-jacket will keep you afloat even when you are unconscious and thus increase your chances; it will also provide some insulation, and reduce heat lost through trying to keep afloat. They should be available on board, and worn either at the owner's insistence or from individual preference.

With all safety equipment a balance must be struck. The only way to be really safe is not to go to sea at all, but assuming one does, it is prudent to take reasonable precautions against disaster. Regulations can insist that you carry certain equipment for emergencies, but only those on the spot can decide how and when to use it. Remember that safety equipment does not stop you getting into trouble: it only helps you to survive once you are in trouble.

Much of the modern electronic equipment fitted to yachts can help to prevent trouble or can assist if it arises. None of it can be considered essential, but yachting is usually undertaken for pleasure, and electronics can go a long way to making passage-making easier and more reliable, and sailing more efficient. The limits are set by the owner's purse and the space and power supply on board. Local regulations may affect installations, equipment specifications and operating procedures.

Radio (i.e. radio telephone with transmitter and receiver) is now a common piece of equipment on yachts. Receivers alone have long been used for weather forecasts, etc. Radio telephones can be either medium frequency (MF) or very high frequency (VHF). Recent international regulations dictating that newly installed (and after a certain date, *all*) MF sets have to be of the expensive single side band (SSB) type, have led to an upsurge in the sales of the smaller and cheaper VHF sets. These are simple to operate and require little power from the batteries; aerial installation is straightforward. In popular sailing waters the VHF set offers the yachtsman a reliable and useful communication aid. The snag with VHF is that the range of transmission is limited to little more than the line of sight between aerials. In practice this means a maximum of around 25 miles for reliable communication. This is adequate for a lot of areas, and most harbour and port authorities use these frequencies; certainly it should be possible to request information or summon assistance if necessary in most coastal areas. Both VHF and MF can be used to make telephone calls to inland telephone sub-scribers in many countries. Calls are made through specified shore stations, and it is here that the limitations of range of VHF become apparent as such shore stations may be fairly widely spaced. Accepting this limitation, VHF can be otherwise very useful in coastal sailing.

For motorsailer owners with a more adventurous disposition, the MF set should be considered in spite of its additional cost, space and power requirements. Such a set should give reliable communication over ranges up to (and perhaps beyond) 200 miles, which should be adequate for the longer open water passages. The peace of mind engendered by being able to talk to stations ashore can be worth the expense. The aerial requirements for a MF set are more complex than for VHF, but in many cases the backstay can be used as an aerial provided that insulators are fitted at the top and bottom. The main drawback is the very much higher cost of SSB equipment.

Logs and echosounders are now almost standard fittings. The displays or dials of both should be positioned so that they can be viewed from any steering position. The speedometer type of log is particularly useful when sailing as it will immediately show the effect of any alteration in the sails. It is not as necessary when under power as it is a simple matter to relate engine r.p.m. to speed, by running over a measured mile at different r.p.m. and drawing a graph of the results. Readings obtained this way will give sufficient accuracy for most navigation purposes, once realistic allowance has been made for the prevailing conditions.

The ultimate in electronic equipment is a radar set. They are relatively expensive, but for the information which they can provide can be very worthwhile. Fitting radar to a motorsailer is usually comparatively simple compared with some boats. Obviously the PPI or display will be sited in the wheelhouse, where it will keep dry and be available to the helmsman. The logical place for the scanner is on the wheelhouse top provided there is adequate clearance under the boom. The totally enclosed type of scanner is best suited to this purpose so that there is no danger of ropes fouling when the scanner is turning. It has even been placed forward of the mast, though this is rare (5.3). On ketches an alternative position for the scanner is on the forward side of the mizzen mast. The equipment will give better results with the scanner mounted higher, but it does add weight high up which will affect stability and windage. This is not usually a problem on motorsailers, where there are usually adequate reserves of stability. The sails will have little effect on the performance of the set and will reflect little or nothing of the radar waves.

The presentation of information on a radar display makes it all too easy to accept everything one sees as reliable information. Unfortunately this is not the case, and it requires considerable experience to interpret the picture properly. Any owner fitting radar for the first time would do well to spend a good deal of time studying the subject closely. Radar can take a lot of the guesswork out of navigation, particularly in bad weather or fog, but its use on small craft for collision avoidance in fog is questionable. This last comment will raise a few eyebrows, but analysis will show this to be the case. To prevent collisions the helmsman must first be aware of all the objects about him. Radar working at complete efficiency will provide this information, but unfortunately radars on small boats rarely work at this level. The big problem is the sea itself: every wave will reflect part of the radar beam and thus show an echo on the screen. The echoes produced by small craft and similar small, low objects are not much stronger than those made by the waves, and they are easily lost among the general sea clutter in the centre of the picture just when you want to know where they are. The rougher the sea the worse the situation becomes, but fortunately fog and rough seas do not *usually* go together. However, one must always be aware of this possible loss of echoes and navigate accordingly. Large ships will always show up, but not the small ones. Wave reflection is reduced, the higher the scanner is placed, and in this respect the ketch rigged boat can score by having it on the mizzen.

Having a radar set does not do away with the need for a radar reflector. Other boats and ships will want to see you on their radar screens, and the chances of this can be greatly improved with a reflector. This should be mounted as high as possible, and be of the rigid type which will not distort in a strong wind. The size of the reflector does have a bearing on its efficiency and the minimum size should be considered as 18 in across.

Radio direction finding (RDF or DF) is another electronic aid to navigation, providing bearings of identifiable radio beacons with varying degrees of accuracy. Small portable sets are available which are fairly cheap and can provide a reasonable check on position when other means are not available. RDF can be very useful for checking positions on long open-water passages, but any landfall made with this information should be treated with great caution. To get the best results a fixed set should be calibrated, and a portable one checked at frequent intervals and used from the same position on the boat all the time.

Part of the challenge of running any yacht is in efficient navigation. There are some very sophisticated electronic instruments which will give a position simply by reading dials. These include Decca Navigator and Loran, but they are a little outside the scope of the average motorsailer, although there are no technical reasons why they cannot be fitted. They take a lot of the guesswork out of navigation, but they *can* fail and one must still carry the basic instruments – a compass and a watch.

The compass is the most important instrument of all and yet one sees some most unsuitable examples being used. It is of little help knowing exactly where you are if you do not know the course to steer. A good, well corrected compass is of prime importance, particularly on long passages where opportunities to check position may be few. A small error in the compass can lead to being a long way out on making a landfall. For the required degree of accuracy not only must the compass be of a suitable type, but positioned

8.1 The after cabin top used as a support for the radar scanner on a sloop. Ketches commonly carry their scanners at the mizzen spreaders on special brackets, but with the disadvantages of added weight and windage aloft, less accessibility for servicing, and the chance of getting lines snagged round them. The lower position gives less satisfactory range and clarity of picture, but is a practical alternative for one mast or where weight is to be kept low; it is also well away from the radar reflector. (Nicholson 42)

and corrected with great care.

Matching the compass to the boat means ensuring that the damping characteristics of the compass card and gimbals, if fitted, are such that the card will not oscillate unduly when the boat pitches and rolls. Manufacturers produce a range of compasses with differing characteristics for various applications, and consultation should produce the right one. I am surprised that many motorsailer builders do not fit a compass as standard, instead of allowing the purchaser to fit one which he prefers. The builder must or should know which type or types of compass behave best in his boat, and an owner could waste both time and money experimenting, or as usually happens, make do with second best.

Compass position is usually clearly dictated by the design of the boat. Almost invariably it is on a shelf above the engine instruments and controls where it can be seen clearly by the helmsman. With the compass having priority it is then necessary to carefully position other equipment in relation to it, so that a minimum of interference is caused. Where it is impossible to remove the compass from electrical or magnetic influences, it may be better to have a remotely sited compass with a repeater unit for the helmsman, and perhaps another for the navigator. Many electrical or magnetic items have a safe distance marked on them and this should be considered an absolute minimum, as all such equipment affects compasses. A constant magnetic field can be corrected, but it is the varying ones which cause problems. Windscreen wipers, radios, radar, echosounders etc are all liable to be switched on or off causing variations in the overall magnetic environment and the only answer is to keep them well away from the compass. The instruments on the dashboard can cause problems in a motorsailer, being activated when the engine is running and passive when sailing; they are also usually close to the compass where their effect may be greater. The best way to check out all the apparatus is to switch each item on separately with the boat on a fixed heading and note whether there is any deflection of the compass card. This should be done on several different headings, and any which do affect the compass to a perceptible degree must either be moved or have a special deviation card made up with the equipment switched on and off.

It is not only equipment in the wheelhouse which affects the compass. Magnetic fields can pass through wood and plastic, which means that anything on the after bulkhead in the amidships accommodation will be very close to the compass in effect even though it is not apparent visually. This is often chosen as the spot for a special shelf for the transistor radio, and such proximity to the compass must be guarded against. Other iron or steel objects such as tools, beer cans, steel-cased batteries and even articles in the helmsman's pocket can also affect the compass. A compass adjustor can remove a lot of the errors and ensure that the instrument performs as expected, but no amount of work on his part will compensate for a spanner left close to the compass.

I have written at some length about compasses because so often they are taken for granted, and they are important. The other basic requirement needed for navigation is time. This can be a simple watch, but it is as well to have at least two on board to ensure reliability. Time is taken so much for granted that one can easily be let down. A good boat's clock is the answer.

Other navigation essentials such as charts, parallel rules, dividers etc are very much in the realm of personal preference. For some, the joy of going to sea is the challenge of navigating, and they will have strong views about their requirements. For others, navigation is more mundane and they will want things as simple and reliable as possible. In the space available on a motor-sailer there is no excuse for sloppy navigation, though one of the difficulties when making an extended passage with a small crew is leaving the wheel to navigate when alone on watch. A lot of pleasure can be gained from motorsailing if an autopilot is fitted: it leaves the helmsman free to move about the wheelhouse and deck, and trim sails, but it does not relieve him of the obligation to keep a proper lookout. The conscientious helmsman can keep a better lookout with the help of an autopilot as he is not affected by any blind spots which may be apparent at the steering position, and can move around so his vision is not through glass.

Autopilots work from the impulses picked up from sensors fitted to a special compass. It can be mounted in any convenient position, given accessibility to set up the required course and lack of magnetic interference – as with an ordinary compass. The impulses, after suitable amplification and conversion, are fed to an electric or hydraulic motor which drives the rudder. Sophisticated autopilots have additional controls whereby the angle of yaw and angle of rudder can be varied so that wind and sea conditions can be taken into account. They are complicated pieces of machinery, but their price is reasonable for what they offer in terms of more pleasurable passage-making. For the motorsailer they are becoming considered almost essential, and this type of yacht must provide one of their biggest markets. They should work equally well when under sail and motor, although there must be a reasonable wind when sailing. They will not take into account any change in the wind direction, but as they do not replace the person on watch this is not important.

For motorsailers, compass-controlled autopilots are much more practical than purely wind-actuated self-steering devices, which keep a boat sailing on a set angle in relation to the wind. They are favoured more on sailing boats, primarily because of their lack of sustained electrical power. While there is usually ample power available on a motorsailer, the autopilot does make a fairly heavy drain on the batteries, and this should be remembered when sailing.

Much of the equipment on modern motorsailers relies on electrical power, and one of the snags of sailing for long periods is that as the batteries are not being charged the drain can be considerable. One way round this problem is to fit an auxiliary generator, normally in the engine compartment and diesel driven so that the same fuel is used as for the main engine. The snag is noise: to have an auxiliary going when under sail spoils a lot of the fun of sailing, and you will not gain many friends if you run it in harbour.

Where the propeller shaft is not braked it is possible to have an alternator belt driven from the shaft. This will take a bit more off the boat's speed as the propeller will be harder to turn, but it will be reasonably quiet. Some form of clutch will still be necessary, otherwise the alternator will turn too quickly when under power, and in light air little, if any, power will be produced. Both of these auxiliary suggestions are gilding the lily a bit, and the vast majority of owners operate within their battery capacity. At many marinas shore power is available, and a rectifier or other converter can make ample power available when tied up.

Any vessel being used at night must have navigation lights to indicate its whereabouts and heading. The International Regula-

8.2   Navigation lights must be absolutely watertight when mounted in this position. The anchor chain could easily jump out of the small shallow rollers on the stemhead fitting. (Lchi/Joemarin 34)

tions for the Prevention of Collision at Sea specify the minimum range at which these should be visible, and certainly the brighter the lights the better. Such lights are very exposed to the weather and should be totally waterproof. On a motorsailer, as with a sailboat, it is not always easy to position navigation lights where they can be seen as required with the sails up. Conventionally, sidelights are now placed either forward on the pulpit or on the wheelhouse top. The latter is only suitable if the sails are set well clear of the deck, but even then they could be obscured when the boat is heeled. The white steaming light usually goes at the masthead or on the forward side of the mast and the stern light on the after side of the wheelhouse or the stern rail. New combined lights which are installed at the masthead cannot be obstructed in any way, and although not strictly within the letter of the Rules, they certainly allow a sailing yacht to be sighted a good way off. Take good care of your lights and let 'see and be seen' be your motto at sea.

Other statutory requirements are a foghorn for use underway, which can be hand, electrically or air driven, and a bell, frying pan or similar instrument to bang when at anchor. A boat proceeding in daylight under motor with sails up, which is often the case with a motorsailer, should show a black conical shape, point down, with a minimum size of 2 ft. I don't think I have ever seen a yacht carry one of these, but that is what the Regulations say.

When cruising one is attracted by many small ports and harbours where a berth alongside is out of the question and the boat has to be anchored or moored. This raises the difficulty of where to stow the dinghy. Rigid dinghies are now almost things of the past, except on some larger motorsailers or power yachts where there is space for stowage. The inflatable is now almost universal, because it can be stowed away safely on long passages, or towed on short ones, and does offer flotation in an emergency.

Stowage of *any* dinghy on deck except for short passages should not be considered unless the motorsailer is large. A dinghy is very difficult to secure on deck adequately, and offers a large area to

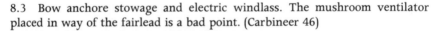

8.3 Bow anchore stowage and electric windlass. The mushroom ventilator placed in way of the fairlead is a bad point. (Carbineer 46)

any sea which might come on board. In most cases it will severely restrict visibility from the helm and generally make a nuisance of itself. An alternative stowage is in davits over the transom, but again this is only practical on larger motorsailers or when very small dinghies are used. The shape and size of the stern rule it out for the majority; there is also the matter of extra expense and windage. Towing astern is fine on short passages in fine weather, but it is no place to have a dinghy when the wind is freshening and the sea getting up. It should not be difficult to find stowage for a deflated dinghy when on passage, either folded and lashed on deck or down below. An outboard is best stowed clamped to a suitable piece of wood in the engine compartment if there is space. Remember these engines run on petrol, so take care there is no chance of leakage.

Anchors, ropes, fenders and other deck gear are largely a matter for common sense. Anchors are usually of such a size to hold the boat securely in a quiet anchorage, but if things should go wrong they may have to be used in open water in a gale of wind, without being too choosy about the type of bottom. This is not so likely in a motorsailer with its alternative means of propulsion, but it behoves one to have an anchor of more than adequate size. A largish anchor, small crew and probably a fair displacement often mean an anchor windlass (winch). These can be hand, electrically or hydraulically operated, and modern ones are very compact in design. They often double up as the forward mooring post, thus avoiding too much clutter on the foredeck. Some types can cope with rope or chain with equal facility.

The list of equipment which can be fitted is endless, but before you rush out and buy things think carefully about what benefit they will bring, where they are going to be fitted or stowed, and what maintenance is required. The last aspect is important, as most equipment requires some sort of attention if it is to continue working efficiently, and if this means bringing in a service agent this can be quite expensive, once the agent has been found. When buying a new boat the equipment and options should be carefully studied, particularly if it is built abroad. It may be impossible to get some of the equipment serviced or obtain spares in your own country, although most builders are very careful in this respect and only fit equipment which is sold and serviced internationally.

9 Handling

One of the great difficulties about boat handling is that it is an operation which takes place in one of the most unpredictable areas for transport, namely at the interface between two fluids, air and water. By contrast, an airplane operates purely in the air, and its behaviour is much more predictable and accounts for the much more scientific approach to design. A boat is always partly in one medium and partly in another, and in the case of the motorsailer, the drive can come from one or the other, or both. In practice it is usually fairly simple. An experienced seaman will react instinctively to a set of circumstances and apply the necessary corrections so that the vessel will behave as he wants it to. The novice can achieve the same results by working things out from basic principles until he too eventually becomes expert. Even the expert can get caught out on occasions by a wrong assessment, but experience will usually show him a way out of his predicament.

Boat handling can be conveniently divided into two categories: calm water manoeuvring and open sea work. The differences are mainly in the effect of waves and wind on the boat, and in harbour there are more hard objects to hit. With a motorsailer there is the added complication of two different forms of propulsion, but if these are considered as forces acting on the boat, the principles are the same.

In harbour any vessel is affected by the wind acting on the areas above water and the resistance of the hull moving through the water; the effect of the wind will vary with its strength and the boat's angle or aspect to the wind. When head to wind, the effect will be simply to slow the boat down and the force will be symmetrical on both sides. If there is a large area forward which the wind can catch (a headsail up or poorly stowed or a high bow) there will be no great effect unless the bow sheers slightly off the wind, whereupon the force of the wind will rapidly increase this sheer. From a steering point of view a boat is unstable with much windage forward. If the windage is aft (the mizzen is up or there is a wheelhouse aft) and the boat sheers this will expose the area aft to the wind, tending to make her head up into the wind again. In the first case the boat is unstable in relation to the wind, as once the sheer starts it will tend to get worse; in the second, the position is stable as the windage will tend to keep it head to wind.

The same situation applies to the underwater parts of a hull. A deep forefoot will tend to accentuate any sheer to the side if the boat is moving ahead. When the underwater area is concentrated aft the boat will be directionally stable when moving ahead. The above and underwater areas have been considered separately here, but in practice they work together and it is the resultant balance which affects the boat's behaviour. This is best seen with the wind on the beam.

In the chapter on sails, reference was made to balance in designing the rig. It applies not only to the sails but also to the hull and superstructure as a whole when handling is being considered. The wind acting on the mast, sails, rigging, superstructure and hull will act through an overall centre of effort which will more or less correspond with the geometrical centre of all these effective areas. Obviously this varies in position depending on what sails are up, but the other factors will be constant, at a given angle to the wind. As said earlier, force acting through the centre of effort will be counteracted by the lateral resistance of the hull acting through its centre of lateral resistance. When sailing, the two points should more or less balance: when motoring, this may not be the case, and on many motorsailers the CE will be ahead of the CLR. Such an imbalance will make the boat's head swing off to leeward but under way is easily counteracted by the rudder.

It is only when coming alongside with the wind on the beam that the effect is really noticeable. At slow speed the rudder has less effect so that any other external force turning the boat will be more apparent. It can be embarrassing when having completed a nicely judged run-in alongside to find the boat's head suddenly taking charge.

A wind from astern will not only increase one's speed but can also affect the steering in the same way as a wind from ahead. Providing the boat is moving ahead and downwind, the effect will be less as the apparent wind will be less, but as with the beam wind it will be more pronounced as the boat slows. In fact, in all cases the wind's effect will be more pronounced at slower speeds, partly because the stabilizing effect of the water on the hull will be less and partly because the counteracting force of the rudder is reduced.

When manoeuvring in harbour, wind is the main external force, in relation to the water. However, the biggest problem is caused by the fact that the water itself is probably moving due to stream and/or current, and it is moving in relation to the fixed object (quay or buoy) which you are making for. It is also moving in relation to shoals, rocks and moored boats and other objects which you are trying to avoid. This presents more of a navigational problem than a handling problem, inasmuch as you have to set a course to counteract the effect of the tide much as one does at sea. In harbour this is usually done by eye rather than on the chart, and there are plenty of objects around on which to check.

Used properly, a current can make handling much easier as it allows the boat to move through the water while it is not moving over the ground. As water flows past it the rudder will still be effective, and with careful judgement the boat can be made to move sideways. Any manoeuvring should always be done against the stream so that this control is maintained, but care must be taken not to use so much helm that the boat gets across it and is then swept bodily sideways. It is only by stemming the stream that the boat can stop in relation to fixed objects, and this point is worth bearing in mind when making harbour in poor visibility. This should only be attempted on the ebb tide, so that if anything is sighted ahead the boat can be stopped completely while it is identified.

In harbour manoeuvring, then, we have the wind and stream as external forces acting on the boat. Internal forces are, or should be, largely under the control of the helmsman; they are the thrust from the engine, sails and rudder. Using these independently or in combinations it should be possible to put the boat where it is wanted.

Propeller thrust can either act forwards or backwards and is simply governed by the action of the throttle and gears. To complicate the situation there is also a sideways component involved in propeller thrust which is particularly noticeable at slow speeds, when the rudder is less able to correct it. With the angled blades of a propeller a sideways thrust is always present on each blade, but in water at depth this is balanced between the blades, the thrust at the top in one direction balancing the thrust at the bottom in the other. For a propeller working just under the surface, the water surrounding the bottom blade is more 'solid' than that around the top, and so the sideways thrust does not balance out. The resultant force acts on the stern to swing it sideways. With a right-handed propeller, as is most commonly fitted, the bow will swing to port when going ahead and to starboard when going astern.

The amount of this sideways thrust or 'kick' will vary both with the size of the propeller and its depth below the surface. On motorsailers where propeller size is fairly large and depth is restricted the effect can be very noticeable, and if used intelligently can assist in handling. In a narrow river it is logical to turn round in the direction where the sideways thrust will assist – all right if the turn can be completed in one go, but if the boat has to back and fill, the sideways thrust will be partially cancelled out by going astern when it acts in the opposite direction. In coming alongside, the effect has to be watched as putting the engine astern to take way off can cause the stern to swing alarmingly. If understood properly, this can be put to good use, particularly when the boat is stopped and has to be turned round short. A quick burst on the engine with the rudder hard over in the required direction can have a large turning effect before the boat gathers headway. The balanced rudders on some motorsailers can help here as they extend over a larger area of the propeller stream.

No two boats are quite the same when it comes to handling, and if it is to be done reliably and successfully the owner and crew should practise under varying conditions of wind and tide. A motorsailer is a heavy boat for its size, and will carry a lot of way after the engine is taken out of gear: it will also take a fair time to pick up speed. Astern power is usually very good, but before trying out any tricky manoeuvres it is no bad thing to make sure that the brakes are working – in other words, that she will go astern.

Bringing a boat into berth or to a mooring under sail alone can be rewarding, and should be within the capabilities of any motorsailer worth its salt. The two main points to remember are the lack of brakes when under sail, and the reduced effect of the steering at slow speeds involved. Any such manoeuvre will depend on there being sufficient wind for the purpose, and account must be taken of the shielding or reflecting effect of buildings nearby. This can be critical if a strong stream is running. The lack of brakes and heavy weight mean that the final approach must be at slow speed and as far as possible with the wind finally from ahead to slow the boat. Slow-speed steering can be assisted by manipulating the sails, and a ketch or yawl rig with small sails at each end of the hull is very good for this. Spilling the wind from jib or mizzen, when the wind is on the beam, can produce a considerable steering effect. When the wind is ahead, perhaps when making the final approach to a berth, steering can be assisted by backing the jib.

Response to the rudder will depend to a large degree on the underwater profile of the hull, assuming that the rudder is adequate for its purpose. The ends of the hull offer maximum resistance to turning: if these are cut away, as on many yachts, then it will turn easily, but if they are full and the keel is long and straight it will be more difficult to turn. It behoves the owner to know his boat well if he is to manoeuvre with confidence, and to consider this aspect when choosing a boat or type of boat.

The same principles apply in handling at sea. It is here that that somewhat undefinable quality of seaworthiness comes in. Once at sea you're stuck with the boat you've got, and apart from battening down and securing there is little that can be done to improve it. From then on it is the seamanship of the helmsman which counts. Most motorsailers are sound, seaworthy boats, and there is little risk of structural failure. Some have large areas of glass in their wheelhouses and some have high coachroofs, wheelhouses or shelters which could be vulnerable: a helmsman must recognize and understand the weak areas in his boat so that he can avoid placing too much strain on them.

The strain on most parts of a boat is increased as speed increases, and it must be driven at a speed to suit the conditions. Comfort will often dictate this, and if your crew are being thrown about in an uncomfortable manner then it is probably an indication that you are driving the boat too hard. Full speed at force 4 should present little discomfort, except perhaps in a head sea when pitching could become a little heavy. If this is the case a small reduction in engine revs should make life more comfortable and reduce spray, with little reduction in speed. Motorsailers generally have excessive power for fine weather work, and the top end of the r.p.m. range tends to increase fuel consumption with very little increase in speed. Because the boat is being forced along at maximum speed it will have little resilience when meeting a wave and will force its way through it. Under slightly less pressure it will yield slightly, and the meeting between wave and hull will be much easier.

In beam and following seas this problem does not arise in moderate sea conditions, although life could be uncomfortable due to excessive rolling. While motorsailers are designed to have good stability under sail, this could be excessive under motor alone, causing sharp rolling. Altering speed will have little effect, although slowing down may increase the rolling. Altering course slightly may help, but the easy solution is to hoist sail, either to help the boat on its way or merely to steady her.

When the wind freshens and the seas get up, the helmsman will want to maintain course as long as possible, but he must recognize when things are getting tough and think of an alteration of course as one of the possibilities open to him. I have already mentioned the discomfort of the crew as one of the signs that a boat is being pressed too hard, and another is if green seas start coming on board. Spray is inevitable as the sea gets up and does little harm except to affect visibility. Solid water is a different matter, and should be avoided as far as possible as it carries the possibility of damaging the boat, and also the risk of being held temporarily on deck or in the cockpit where the weight could have a consider-able effect of stability.

In such conditions the prudent person will start looking at alternatives. The first thing is to try to get an accurate weather forecast so that one has as sound a basis as possible on which to base a decision. Don't take the forecast as gospel, but try to relate it to prevailing conditions. With experience, this can provide much more accurate estimates of the timing of changes, which you are primarily interested in.

The alternatives in bad weather are to press on to the destination if this is not too far away, to seek shelter until the sea moderates, to adopt a course which is less demanding of boat and crew, or to heave to. Pressing on has the attraction of completing what you set out to do, and a well found motorsailer should be capable of this unless things are very bad. But judgement tends to become clouded by the lure of the haven ahead, and this is where things can start to go wrong. There is also the risk that the prevailing conditions may have made its entrance dangerous.

Seeking shelter behind a suitable piece of land or even a shoal can give a respite until conditions moderate, and this is probably the most prudent course if such shelter is near at hand, and it is possible to maintain position in the sheltered area. It does demand a knowledge of the future weather pattern as a wind shift can turn a usable anchorage into an exposed lee shore in a short time.

The last two alternatives are adopted in the open sea when shelter is not available. Altering course still enables progress to be made in a direction hopefully somewhere near the original, while reducing both the motion and the strain on the boat. A motorsailer with a powerful engine should permit any course to be adopted in bad conditions without fear of losing control as can happen with underpowered vessels. The relative merits of different courses will depend a great deal on conditions at the time and on the proximity of any dangers.

Heading into the seas requires delicate control of the throttle to avoid violent pitching and the risk of shipping solid water. The speed must always be maintained so that the rudder is fully effective, and as conditions get bad this may not always be possible. Taking the seas slightly off the bow will have the effect of lengthening their wavelength and slowing pitching, thus enabling satisfactory speed and control to be maintained. It may be prudent to head into the sea if a breaking wave approaches, then allow the bow to fall off again after the wave has passed.

The good stability of the normal motorsailer with a ballast keel does allow safe progress with the seas on the beam, although the motion may be very uncomfortable. Adequate speed must be maintained to give full control and a careful watch kept for breaking waves. Beam-on, a motorsailer is exposing its large super-structure to the waves and a breaking wave hitting from this angle could cause structural damage. Waves rarely break along long fronts except in shoal areas, and it should be possible to head partly into a wave before it breaks to reduce the impact.

Running under power before a sea is not recommended unless there is the prospect of shelter close at hand. A displacement motorsailer has no way of travelling faster than the waves and so will be open to attack from the stern, which is usually one of the most vulnerable areas. On all other courses one can head up into the seas or otherwise reduce the impact if a large breaking wave is seen. When running there is little one can do except hold tight and pray. This is not strictly true, because one will be working hard to maintain a straight course in front of the breaking wave so that it will pass each side of the boat and hopefully not swing it round into a broach. The object is to maintain full steering control, helped by easing the throttle before the wave and then opening it fully as it strikes. This gives additional thrust on the rudder at the critical time, and as the boat is accelerating will reduce the impact of the wave.

Running before a sea can be an exhilarating experience, but a lot depends on the boat. Motorsailers with pointed cruiser sterns and long straight keels are probably best equipped for safe progress. The stern divides the seas and allows them to pass on each side without imparting too much additional speed to the boat or tending to slew it round, whereas the long keel gives good directional stability. A full bow will give plenty of lift to balance the lift of the stern by approaching waves. Broad transom sterns (as on power cruisers) are less manageable; however, because they give greater interior space they are also found on motorsailers (3.3, 7.1).

The foregoing suggestions have been in the context of using the motor only. Having both power and sails in useful proportions means that by combining the two under adverse conditions it is possible to improve the behaviour of a boat. Sails can perform three functions: giving headway, damping the movement of the hull, and steering. Used intelligently they can take a lot of the strain off boat and crew.

Using sails to make much additional headway is not likely as speed is considerably reduced anyway. However, they can enable the engine to be run at lower revs, thus saving fuel and allowing a larger proportion of the engine power to be kept in reserve until a quick reaction to the steering is required. Damping the movement of the hull is one of their biggest attractions. The improvement in comfort on board can be very marked. Food can be prepared where this would otherwise be impossible; navigation is done with more care and accuracy; rest and sleep become easier. Any use of sails for steering is more on the basis of stabilizing the steering and reducing the strain on the helmsman than actual steering.

In bad weather ketch rig has more to offer than sloop rig because of the greater flexibility in choosing sail combinations. In many cases it can obviate the need to reef, sail area being reduced by simply taking one or more sails down. With a small sail left at each end of the boat, the wind can be used to maximum advantage to achieve the desired balance.

Heading into a sea the sails will not hold any wind, but can still exert a certain stabilizing effect, providing one doesn't mind the noise. Maintaining such a heading will be made easier with the sail area aft, and the mizzens often seen on fishing boats are for the purpose of keeping these boats head to wind when fishing. With the wind on the bow the sails will just hold the wind and increase headway. They will considerably ease the motion, but cause heeling. Under these conditions only a mizzen or reefed main is recommended to give the required stability without too much heeling. With the centre of effort well aft, the boat will naturally tend to point up into the wind, which is desirable if a really big wave comes along.

With the wind on the beam the steering can be biased as desired by suitable sail balance. The heeling tendency will be greatest at this angle to the wind, as will rolling induced by the waves, and this may become excessive in a heavy sea. Breaking waves hitting a boat heeled excessively to leeward have been known to cause considerable damage, and a course more into or off the wind would appear preferable to reduce rolling, if progress has to be made in this direction.

In a following wind and sea, a sail can be used to enhance the directional stability so necessary. A headsail pulling at the bow will tend to keep it downwind and lessen the chances of a broach, or help in recovery. The centre of effort of such a sail will be high above the deck and as such will tend to drive the bow down, which is not desirable, but the full bows of most motorsailers should be able to cope with this. The mizzen should not be used.

Having both a powerful engine and efficient smaller sails gives one means to cope with most situations, in particular bad weather. In the event of total engine failure one still has the sails, and though the ability to make good a desired course may be limited, adequate progress should be made. The ability of some motor-oriented motorsailers to beat off a lee shore may be questionable, but otherwise the motorsailer can be treated as an ordinary sailing cruiser.

The poor closehauled ability of some of the motor-oriented types is due partly to the directional stability imparted by the long keel which makes tacking more difficult but more by the excessive leeway which the relatively shallow draft allows, and sometimes low rigs with small sail areas. Tacking can be helped by backing the jib as the boat comes through the wind or by balancing the rig so that the boat naturally comes up into the wind. Little can be done about leeway, although the problem is recognized and one or two boats are fitting centreboards to improve lateral resistance. The remedy is neither easy nor cheap, however.

Most of the foregoing comments about bad weather apply to conditions up to about force 8, where progress (albeit slow progress) can still be made but the boat has to be nursed. In a force 9 or 10 one is more intent on survival than progress, and different tactics have to be adopted. Again, the action taken will depend largely on the prevailing conditions and sea room. With limited sea room to leeward or the proximity of rocks, shoals or tidal races, one has little alternative but to try to make progress. The motorsailer with its strong hull and rig and its powerful engine is as well equipped as most boats to do this. Given plenty of sea room, one is left with the alternatives of heaving to, lying a-hull, lying to a sea anchor, or running with warps trailing. Heaving-to involves setting a minimum of sail, or running the engine at slow speed, or both; jogging along, if that is the right term, with the wind some five to six points on the bow. Life can be very uncomfortable under these conditions, but you still have control. Hove-to under motor alone one could head closer into the wind, thus presenting the strongest part of the boat to the sea, but steerage way would have to be maintained.

Lying a-hull is really taking the easy way out. It means taking down all sail, stopping the engine, battening everything down securely and letting the boat sort the problem out. Providing she is strong enough this can prove very satisfactory as it reduces the stress on the crew and the boat tends to give to the waves rather than to fight them. It may be necessary to cover up all windows as far as possible and strengthen any weaknesses in the superstructure such as wheelhouse doors. The boat will normally adopt an attitude nearly beam-on to the seas, and when a wave strikes will heel and tend to slide to leeward. The weight of the ballast keel will ensure that the boat rights itself, though knockdowns and even rolling over when a-hull have been known. This course should be satisfactory on boats up to about 40 ft in length; above this, the weight of the boat will make it less resilient and it may offer too much resistance to the waves, causing damage.

One hears of sea anchors put out forward as the panacea for all the evils of rough seas, at least in theory. In practice hardly any boats carry them, and the chances of rigging one successfully are remote under rough conditions. Books on rough sea sailing even advocate constructing a sea anchor from spare materials which are handy, but I think that these advocates can have had little experience in small boats in very rough conditions.

If you don't like the idea of letting the boat do all the work and you want to retain some control, then by trailing long warps the stern will be brought into the wind and she will run before the sea under bare poles. The rudder will be effective to give added control. This method has been used successfully in sailing boats, but with a powerful engine available, it could be preferable to heave-to under power.

It is not an easy choice to make, and so much depends on the boat in question, the amount of fuel, sea room, and last but not least, the strength of the crew. An owner should think about these conditions and prepare for them mentally and materially in case he is caught out. Maintenance must never be neglected, as failure of some part is usually part of the story of every disaster.

Coming back to lighter things, a motorsailer will spend a good deal of its time at sea with both the engine running and the sails set. This combination saves fuel and makes life on board more comfortable by reducing rolling. When the engine is driving the boat, wind is produced which is equal to its speed but opposite in direction: combination with the actual wind produces the apparent wind. The effect is to reduce the efficiency of the sails, as the apparent wind draws ahead, and so one gains less effect from the sails than would be expected.

In a following sea the apparent wind acting on the sails will be the actual wind less the speed of the boat, and in a light wind it may not even fill the sails. On a reach, the effect will be less noticeable, the main differences being that the direction of the apparent wind will be more ahead. The same applies when close-hauled, so that in effect a motorsailer with the engine running will not be able to point as close to the true wind. As the wind strengthens the difference in direction between the true and apparent wind lessens. Looked at another way, motorsailing necessitates a rig which is more close-winded than is often assumed, otherwise performance is reduced. Again, this aspect is one to be considered by the prospective owner.

10 Future Developments

To try to anticipate the future is to invite criticism, yet this is the way to progress. Yachting is a leisure pursuit for all but a few participants and therefore development does not necessarily follow a rational path. It is much more open to the whims and fancies of fashion and the individual. As mass production of boats grows, as it surely must, there will be less scope for individual taste apart from the fortunate few who can afford custom boats.

The worry is that when boats are built for the majority market we may find that the majority of owners stay in harbour rather than venture to sea. If boats reflect this trend, then they will end up as water caravans, with all of the bad taste and loss of standards which that phrase implies. The motorsailer has developed along strong functional and seamanlike lines up to now, and it is to be hoped that its future development will continue this trend. By filling in the gap between the motor cruiser and the auxiliary sailing yacht, the motorsailer has now developed into a boat with an identity of its own. No longer is it looked on as the poor relation, as the boat where its designer has tried to achieve the impossible and make a type which will both sail and motor well.

The motorsailer will become the cruising boat of the future. One can visualize pure motor boats being restricted to planing types where speed is important, and pure sailing boats being restricted to the all-out racing machines. Similar specialization is occurring with motorsailers as their sailing vs power orientation shows. I am overlooking the possibility that future motorsailers may be capable of attaining planing speed. Making such a hull capable of planing under power is a lot closer, and already some modern designs are exceeding the maximum speeds they should be capable of as pure displacement hulls.

One of the big difficulties in making any hull go faster is in reducing the wetted surface area. To get good closehauled performance under sail, there must be a good immersed depth to reduce leeway, and this is one area where the requirements of motor and sail conflict in today's motorsailers, as minimum or moderate draft is a requirement for cruising. Centreboards are slowly returning to favour as a means of varying draft. There was always the risk of the board jamming up or down, and leaks from the case were often a problem. Modern designs include the centreboard in the keel, and hydraulic rams are used to raise and lower the board. This reduces the chance of jamming as the board is pushed down rather than relying on gravity.

If weight has to be reduced to enable a boat to get lift from the water so that it can plane, then the required stability will have to be found in other ways. A large proportion of the weight of any sailing yacht goes towards keeping it upright. The alternative is to increase the beam, but this then increases wetted surface, which is self-defeating. One way of increasing beam without increasing wetted surface is to use the catamaran configuration. The speed potential of cats is well known, and is achieved partly through reduction in weight (since no ballast is required) and partly through the narrowness of the individual hulls which enables them to operate at higher speeds without creating the restricting wave patterns of beamier hulls. Logically, the catamaran is potentially the most advanced motorsailer on the market today, offering a performance under both sail and motor which far exceeds that of the conventional single-hulled type.

While catamarans have made many ocean crossings and proved themselves in many other ways there have been many well-publicized incidents involving capsizes or hulls breaking up, and this has left a big question mark in many people's minds. I feel that much of this lack of confidence in the catamaran is caused by

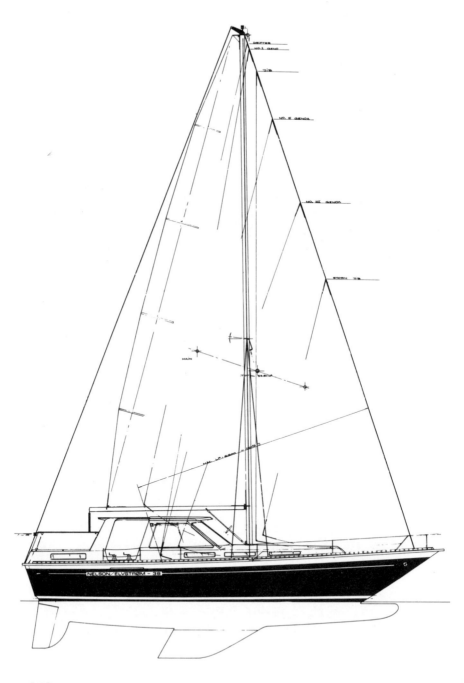

examples of amateur construction which perhaps left something to be desired. The production catamarans now appearing offer a more practical approach to the problem and have avoided the pitfall of trying to make everything as light as possible to maximize speed.

There is no doubt that the future will see the catamaran emerge as a serious cruising boat. With its excellent performance under sail with an engine in each hull it will offer safe and exciting cruising. The large deck area can be an attraction in warm climates, but the accommodation layout dictated by the hull configuration is not to everyone's taste, and is probably what puts people off the catamaran as a motorsailer more than any other factor.

The vast majority of motorsailers built today have hulls and superstructures made from fibreglass. There is no doubt that this material has revolutionized boatbuilding, and now it is only the one-off or larger craft which are built in wood. Steel has a limited application for small motorsailer design, and the hulls tend to look angular unless a lot of expense is incurred in forming and filling curved shapes. Even fibreglass is starting to get very expensive due to the increased cost of raw materials, and the future may see the increased use of ferrocement. It is an ideal material for the traditional motorsailer where weight is not too critical. A finished hull compares favourably in weight with a fibreglass hull, but can be considerably cheaper. Like so many new materials, the amateur constructor has used it first, and some bad examples have given the material a dubious reputation. Ferrocement is now at the stage

---

10.1   The Nelson/Elvström 38, remarkable for a 'ram bow' designed to reduce drag, in particular at the upper end of the boat's speed range but to a degree over the whole range. The bulbous bow principle has been adopted for some time in ship construction, but pitching, heeling, yawing, a broad speed range and the very different underwater form of sailing craft make it a complex design problem. The shape and position are critical, and an even slightly wrong bulb is more detrimental than a traditional stem. The designers, Paul Elvström and Jan Kjaerulff, developed it in the course of testing 12 and 6 Metre designs; within limits, the relevant rules for those boats do not penalize bulbs, whereas the IOR does. The tall rig carries a working sail area (main and jib) of 570 sq ft (51 m^2) and the engine is a 75 h.p. Volvo Penta diesel.

that fibreglass was roughly fifteen years ago, while gradually gaining acceptance as a worthwhile boatbuilding material. The standard of finish is improving, and mass-production methods are being devised which should produce a thoroughly reliable product.

Engines have developed enormously over the past two decades and it is this more than anything else which has made the small motorsailer a viable proposition. The advent of lightweight high-powered diesels has provided adequate power in a small compact unit without introducing undue weight. The next generation of marine engine is likely to be the gas turbine, and these are being developed in quite low horsepowers for small craft. The planing motorsailer could become a reality if such units were available, allowing plenty of power in a compact, lightweight installation. At present cost is something like ten times that of an equivalent diesel engine, however.

Propellers are an area where much improvement can be made in reconciling an efficient propeller with the drag it causes when under sail. Variable pitch propellers which can be completely feathered when sailing are available, their main drawback being that they are very expensive. No gearbox is required, however, which makes the cost more reasonable. There are examples of variable pitch propellers on a few larger motorsailers, but the idea has not caught on in the smaller boats yet. There is a slight loss of power with a variable pitch propeller, but with the adequate engines generally found in motorsailers, there is no real problem.

Boat design is a process of gradual development with designers, builders and owners trying out idea in the hope of improvement. Most of the developments mentioned in this chapter have been or are being tried out; many will find acceptance eventually, the overriding factor generally being cost. Whichever way these developments go, there is no doubt that the motorsailer as a first class cruising boat is here to stay.

Some
Current Designs

The motorsailers shown on the following pages give some idea of the wide range of production boats on the market. The examples are from many different countries and are intended to cover as wide a selection of different types as possible. The intention has been to include those which illustrate a particular aspect or approach to motorsailing, not necessarily the best of a type.

For production boats the approach has to be commercial. The builder hopes to find a gap in the existing range which he can exploit; alternatively, he can try to produce a design which offers a better compromise than his competitors'. All of those shown here are production boats because they represent a more rationalized approach to design.

Editor's note While every effort has been made to obtain correct and current data for the following section, there may be errors, and some figures can only be given as approximations. Engines, tankages, sail areas and accommodation layouts can change on production boats, in the light of experience or buyers' preferences. Displacement, tankage and ballast weights are generally only available in round figures, and where they are stated more precisely by builders it may be more realistic to regard them as round figures.

Banjer

Very much a motor-oriented design along the lines of traditional North Sea fishing boats, the Banjer still represents a fibreglass yacht employing modern materials. At 36 ft (11 m) it is one of the largest clearly motor-oriented production motorsailers. (Above this size the balance between motor and sails tends to become more even.) It is only the inclusion of ballast that orients it towards sailing; otherwise this is largely a motor boat hull.

In plan view, the bow and stern are almost symmetrical with straight topsides. The sections at both bow and stern are very full, and there is no flare at the bow. The design relies on the high freeboard to keep spray down, and the rubbing strake would tend to peel water away from the hull should it become immersed that deeply. In profile the hull shows a pronounced sheerline. The forefoot is deep and joins a long straight keel which slopes aft, with a difference of over a foot between the draft forward and aft. This improves the steering characteristics and should make the boat behave better in a following sea. In a head sea the bow would tend to be blown off the wind more easily, but this would be compensated for by the high wheelhouse aft. Although the long straight keel promotes directional stability, the fact that it slopes up forward allows the boat to turn more readily. It handles well under power, aided by the balanced rudder working in the thrust of the large propeller to give a good turning moment (6.2).

Under sail, performance is poor except in a strong breeze, but the stability and low CE are such that sail could be carried under most conditions. When tacking, she is slow to come through the wind because of the hull shape and in many cases the jib has to be backed to help the bow round. With an (unladen) displacement of around 27,000 lb (12,200 kg) this is not surprising. However, there are several alternative sailplans for the Banjer, apart from the gaff ketch version shown in the photograph. The two largest achieve greater efficiency as well as sail area with the addition of either a stub bowsprit or a longer bowsprit, two headsails and taller masts (see profile drawings). The ketch rig (in all versions) keeps weight low down and the areas of individual sails to manageable proportions. Simplicity is the keynote of the rigging and the sails can almost be left to their own devices when maneouvring. The booms are high in order to clear the wheel-house, and the mainsheet is attached to the boom just aft of its midpoint so that the sheet tackle clears the forward end of the

wheelhouse. Tan sails complement the traditional appearance.

The engine now supplied is a six-cylinder Perkins 6-354 diesel with a maximum continuous rating at 2,400 r.p.m. of 95 h.p. (115 h.p. intermittent one-hour rating at 2,800 r.p.m.). The drive is taken through a 3:1 reduction gearbox to a large 30 or 32 in (0.76 or 0.80 m) three-bladed propeller. While there is a thrust bearing, there is no shaft brake. Such a large propeller produces considerable drag while sailing, but this is a boat primarily designed for motoring or motor-sailing and a propeller of this size is very efficient. The full hull sections allow the shaft to be almost horizontal. Fuel tankage of 350 Imp gal (420 US gal or 1,600 litres) gives a cruising range of over 2,000 miles under power; water tankage is 200 Imp gal (240 US gal or 900 litres). The present power and fuel capacity specification represents some change from the earlier Banjers.

The Banjer is offered with either an open after cockpit or an after cabin. The cockpit is spacious and a door gives direct access to the fully enclosed wheelhouse on the same level. In the after cabin version the coachroof intrudes on the after deck space; access is from inside the wheelhouse making the interior totally enclosed. There is plenty of headroom in the wheelhouse, which is over the engine. Tongue-and-grooved varnished woodwork maintains the traditional effect, and the wheelhouse also has a very functional and practical air. A good chart table is provided, but is mounted awkwardly over the access to the after cabin and has to be folded up. From the wheelhouse visibility is good except of the sails; they are largely hidden from the helmsman, but an extra window can be fitted in the wheelhouse roof to give a view upwards. Most of the other windows open.

Down below, the traditional panelling is continued, and set off by many brass fittings: it gives a very comfortable ambience, but at the expense of light. The after cabin layout has a total of eight berths, versus six in the cockpit version. Four berths are in the main saloon, including a starboard pilot berth which should be very comfortable at sea, the high leeboard giving ample security.

The galley is in its own compartment forward of the saloon and divided from it by a half-bulkhead. Though comprehensively equipped, its situation fairly well forward could make it difficult to entice the cook to produce meals at sea. Hot water is piped from a gas water heater in the galley to the toilet compartments and wash basins in the forward and after cabins, an example of the complexity of the plumbing systems sometimes found on modern motorsailers. A diesel oil-fired heater in the engine compartment supplies hot air to all the cabins and the wheelhouse, making this a boat for use all the year round.

The Banjer has the ability to cruise the oceans of the world, and a hull form to weather the worst conditions. In this respect she is a true motorsailer, but with the accent placed strongly on motoring.

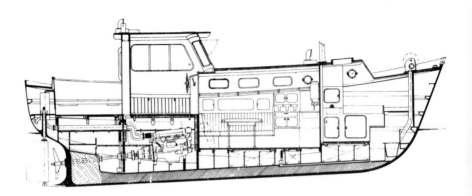

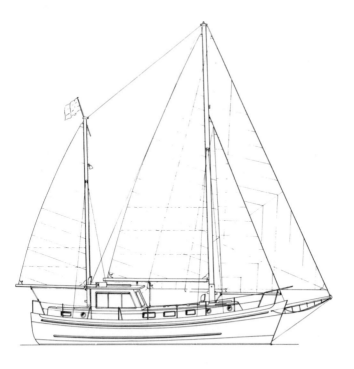

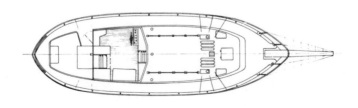

LOA	36′ 6″	11.1 m	Alternative rigs of	320/430/540/860 ft^2
LWL	33′	10.1 m		30/40/50/80 m^2
Beam	11′ 5″	3.5 m	Engine	Perkins 6-354 diesel
Draft	4′ 7″	1.4 m	Fuel	350 Imp gal/420 US gal/1,600 litres
Displ	27,000 lb	12,200 kg	Water	200 Imp gal/240 US gal/900 litres
Ballast	8,800 lb	4,000 kg	Waste	20 Imp gal/24 US gal/90 litres

Built by Eista Werf BV, Nederhemert, Netherlands; designed by Le Feber.

Carbineer 46

The Carbineer 46 is a British quality production motorsailer capable of extended ocean cruising with considerable comfort. The fibreglass hull is developed from sailing cruisers, but like power craft has a large flat transom and a flare and knuckle on the bow. The transom extends almost to the waterline and allows full sections aft above the waterline, making for a spacious after cabin. The stern has a slightly cut-off look balanced by placing the wheelhouse well forward, which gives a pleasing overall appearance.

The bow sections are moderately full to balance the full stern, and the knuckle close under the deck successfully deflects the bow wave outwards, keeping the deck dry even when heeled. Placing this knuckle high up avoids any sudden changes in the shape of the underwater sections which could give rise to uncomfortable pitching. Motion is also smoothed by the full forefoot, which allows the bow sections to be kept full.

The beam is fairly narrow in relation to the length, which allows the hull to be more easily driven but reduces the inherent transverse stability. This is compensated for by a high ballast ratio: ballast accounts for over one-third of the total weight and is placed low down for maximum effect. The draft of 6 ft (1.8 m) is fairly deep for a motorsailer of this size and indicative of how the Carbineer 46 has been designed primarily for working well under sail.

The shortish keel should give good manoeuvrability, and the rudder mounted on a separate skeg aft of the propeller follows current sailing yacht practice. The rudder is not balanced, but the skeg in front of it will improve steering, particularly under power, by providing an additional surface for the propeller thrust to react against. The skeg also gives some protection to the rudder blade and shaft.

Two steering positions are arranged. The outside position is right aft in a shallow cockpit, giving full view of the sails and

deck. Though exposed, some protection could be effected by fitting canvas dodgers on the lifelines. The inside position is completely protected and offers carpet slipper comfort, but the view forward is restricted by the bulwarks, and of the sails only the jib is visible.

The low bulwarks effectively increase the freeboard, and on a hull of this length they do not upset the proportions as might happen on a shorter boat. Bulwarks combined with lifelines make an effective safeguard against going overboard. Wide side decks make moving about easy and safe, except around the wheelhouse where no handholds are fitted.

In motorsailer terms the mainmast is high and necessitates the high ballast ratio. The area of the single headsail ketch rig is sufficient to give good performance even with the standard sails. The basic working jib is set on a boom within the foretriangle and makes handling easy. Optional sails include a genoa and a staysail. Both can greatly enhance performance in light winds, and for anyone taking their sailing seriously they are almost essential. Halyard and sheet winches are also standard.

The CQR anchor is stowed by being hauled up tight into a shaped bow fairlead which holds it securely (8.3). An electric anchor winch is also standard. On a boat of this size, mechanization is essential as the weight of the anchor and size and windage of the boat would make it difficult to haul in by hand, and impossible in some conditions.

The wheelhouse is lavishly equipped, and lined with teak joinery, giving an air of luxury. There is space for all of the crew and meals would be taken there. It also serves as the navigation area.

The galley has been designed for use on long passages, and is in a separate compartment to minimize distraction for the cook or the rest of the crew. Natural light is limited (as elsewhere in the accommodation) because of the deliberate avoidance of large, vulnerable areas of glass, but much attention has been given to the ventilation of the interior, though there is no overall system for the whole boat. Galley equipment is comprehensive, including twin sinks and a hand water pump to supplement the electric tap.

The owner's cabin aft (with its own toilet compartment) is really luxurious and in keeping with the use for which this boat has been designed. In a length of 46 ft (14 m) there are only berths for six, and within the space provided the six people could cruise with great comfort even on long passages.

Power is provided by a Perkins 6-354 six-cylinder diesel producing 95 h.p. at a maximum continuous rating at 2,400 r.p.m. (115 h.p. intermittent one-hour rating at 2,800 r.p.m.). It is on flexible mounts and drive to the propeller is via an intermediate shaft with universal joints. However, it is surprising to find that on a boat of this quality with its obvious orientation towards sailing and capability for making long passages, there is no propeller shaft brake. The fuel capacity is 220 Imp gal (260 US gal or 990 litres) in two separate tanks which should give a cruising range of around 150 hours at 7 knots; a range of about a thousand miles without allowing for any contribution from the sails. The fuel tanks are installed each side of the engine, and the two 90 Imp gal (110 US gal or 410 litres) water tanks are mounted forward of the engine.

The Carbineer is a motorsailer in which a fairly orthodox concept is carried out to a high standard. The finish and equipment are very good, and the temptation to squeeze too much into the space available has been resisted. She can be easily handled by two people, yet could comfortably accommodate six on long passages.

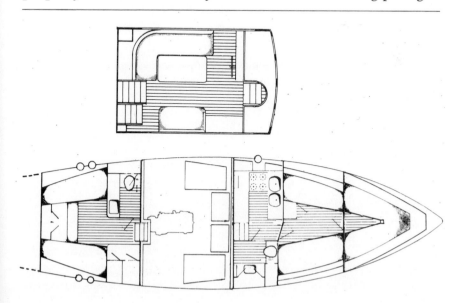

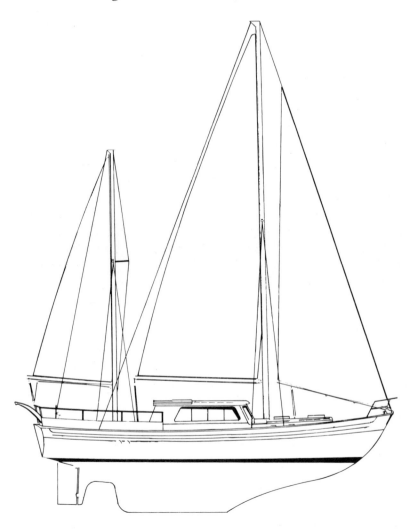

LOA	46' 6"	14.2 m	Sail areas:	main	346 ft^2	32 m^2
LWL	36'	11 m		jib	360 ft^2	34 m^2
Beam	12' 2"	3.7 m		mizzen	145 ft^2	14 m^2
Draft	6'	1.8 m	Engine	Perkins 6-354 diesel		
Displ	36,400 lb	16,500 kg	Fuel	220 Imp gal/260 US gal/1,000 litres		
Ballast	12,600 lb	5,700 kg	Water	90 Imp gal/110 US gal/410 litres		

Built by A H Moody & Son Ltd, Lower Swanwick, Southampton, UK; designed by Laurent Giles & Partners.

Caribbean 35

The Chris-Craft Caribbean represents an American approach to production motorsailer design. There is considerable emphasis on comfort and space down below, with less concern with weather protection above deck. Certainly a sailing-oriented boat, it motors very adequately as well.

Under water the hull follows conventional lines with good draft contributing to sailing performance. It enables ballast to be carried well down and this combined with generous beam gives the stability required to carry a good sail area. For a sailing-oriented motorsailer the displacement is fairly high, but the adequate sail area should mean that little performance is lost.

The hull has a fairly high freeboard which gives a somewhat 'dumpy' look; height is emphasized by the contrasting toerail, and a stronger line lower down the hull would have been an improvement. The effect is further emphasized by the coachroof: from being low forward it rises in a sloping step to form a large bulk over the saloon and forward of the raised cockpit. The heavily cambered coachroof top softens the lines and the designer has resisted the temptation to fit a permanent wheelhouse which would have completely spoiled the proportions. Instead there is a folding spray hood.

The cockpit sole is high, almost at deck level. While this allows usable accommodation space underneath, noise from the crew in the cockpit must intrude on those in the after cabin if they are trying to sleep. A folding spray hood at the forward end of the cockpit has a clear panel to give visibility forward. It gives a certain amount of weather protection, but the cockpit layout is designed basically for the hardy, or for warm climates and summer sailing.

The high coachroof and deep hull combine to give plenty of space below, and the high cockpit sole allows direct access to the after cabin from the main saloon via a short passageway beside the engine compartment, rather than via the cockpit. This gives the effect of a much larger boat and makes living on board very

comfortable. No attempt has been made to cram in as many sleeping berths as possible: the intention has been to provide comfortable living accommodation with reasonable privacy for two couples, and the designer has succeeded. There are two berths in the after cabin and two forward, and each compartment has its own toilet and washing facilities. The large saloon amidships contains the comprehensively equipped galley. Surprisingly there is no refrigerator; only an icebox, but this is quite practical in America or wherever ice supplies are plentiful (they can be prepared in the home food freezer). An icebox does not drain the battery or require any fuel, always works, and is quite adequate for short cruises.

When the boat is used for its intended complement of four the spacious saloon is likely to be used purely as a social area and for eating. However, the dinette does convert into a double berth if additional guests come along. There is plenty of stowage space on board, not only for clothes and personal effects but also for the boat's equipment. The lazarette between the after cabin and the transom provides stowage for all the sails and other deck gear.

The engine is a Perkins 4-108 diesel giving a maximum of around 47 h.p. which is rather on the low side for a boat of this displacement. However, the hull is easily driven and the power adequate for most purposes. Fuel tankage of 80 US gal (66 Imp gal or 300 litres) is enough for most cruising, especially as the boat sails well.

The standard rig is a sloop with a high aspect ratio mainsail. The working foresail fits within the foretriangle, and a genoa is supplied as standard. This gives good performance which can be enhanced by the (optional extra) spinnaker.

For those requiring a more versatile rig, the Caribbean 35 is also available as a ketch, which gives a larger sail area with the standard sails, the mizzen mast being accommodated by a shorter main boom and reduced mainsail foot length. To balance the sails, a short bowsprit is fitted to enable the jib to be larger and farther forward.

Apart from any sailing advantages, the ketch rig improves the appearance; the bowsprit and the mizzen boom projecting aft have a lengthening effect, bringing the coachroof into much better proportion. This is a case where the optional extra really ought to be the standard to make for a good cruising boat. Like so many good things, it puts costs up, and manufacturers are constantly working to a competitive price. At least the alternative is available here if you can pay for it.

Altogether the Caribbean 35 is a comfortable cruising boat where the design has been approached logically without any attempt being made to squeeze the last ounce out of the compromises required. There is still sufficient scope left for the owner to give the boat its own particular character, and this is necessary in a design which is slightly lacking in character as it is handed over to the customer.

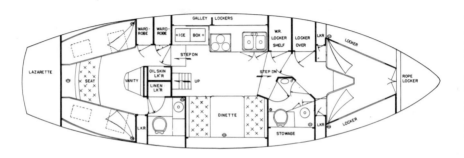

LOA	35′ 2″	10.7 m	Sail areas:	sloop	577 ft²	54 m²
LWL	28′ 6″	8.7 m		ketch	(no figures available)	
Beam	11′	3.4 m	Engine	Perkins 4-108 diesel		
Draft	4′ 8″	1.4 m	Fuel	80 US gal/66 Imp gal/300 litres		
Displ	18,000 lb	8,000 kg				
Ballast	5,000 lb	2,300 kg				

Built by Chris-Craft Corp., Pompano Beach, Florida, USA.

Coaster

While the Coaster is a traditionally based design derived from motor fishing craft, many subtle refinements and modern materials improve its performance as a yacht. With such origins one would expect this to be very definitely motor-oriented, yet its sailing qualities are such that it is very much a true motor-sailer with creditable performance under both power and sail.

In keeping with its origins the 33 ft fibreglass hull has generally full lines, but the underwater sections have been fined down by including a knuckle just above the waterline. It extends from forward to nearly amidships, and combined with the curved forefoot makes a fine entry; the hull is easily driven, yet has plenty of reserve buoyancy. At the bow the knuckle is fairly pronounced and deflects spray or waves outwards. At the same time the increase to full sections above the knuckle while giving good buoyancy could also make the pitching motion in a head sea somewhat jerky.

The stern terminates in a fairly fine section to complement the bow, and similarly flares out above the waterline. The midship sections are full, turning in to the keel with a moderate curve. The forefoot runs down in a gentle curve to a long straight keel. The rudder, mounted on top and bottom bearings, is large for the size of boat, balanced to improve steering, and should compensate for the resistance to turning of the long keel. The three-bladed propeller is in an aperture cut in the deadwood immediately forward of the rudder. It is mounted high in relation to the keel, and while this means working in the more disturbed water nearer the surface, the shaft line is nearly horizontal.

The sheerline is pronounced, with a powerful sweep up to the bow and an upturn at the stern, the lowest point being near the cockpit. Low bulwarks are in a contrasting colour except at bow and stern: this reduces the effect of bulk and gives the hull a very practical and seaworthy appearance. The bulwarks also moderate the effect of the high coachroof. A slightly incongruous note is

184

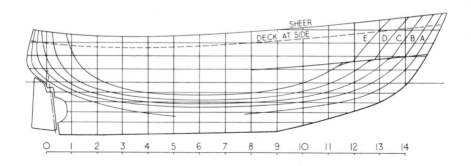

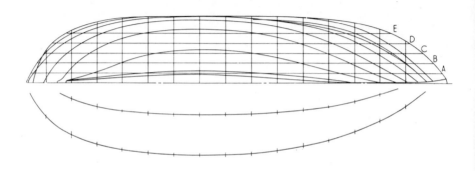

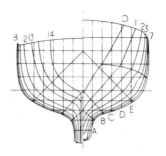

struck by the wheel shelter, which extends both forward and aft of its supports and rather spoils the otherwise good looks of the boat. The extension aft is practical in as much as it offers more protection to the cockpit crew; the extension forward only serves to obstruct the sails from the helmsman's view. A hatch in the wheelhouse top compensates somewhat.

One surprising aspect of the Coaster is the low engine power. On a boat displacing 8 tons (9 US or 8 metric tons) a 31 h.p. unit (continuous rating at 3,000 r.p.m.), normally a Newage/BMC Captain diesel, is barely adequate to give good performance in adverse conditions. The speed of 7.5 knots would drop considerably in a head sea and wind. The hull is obviously motor-oriented, and this size of engine cannot take full advantage of a form which is obviously capable of absorbing considerably more power. However, other units have been installed successfully in various Coasters and there is scope for alternatives.

On the other hand, there is an efficient rig and comparatively large sail area. Ketch rig is used with no extra sails listed as options. The large jib supplied as standard could make it difficult to retain a balanced rig when the time comes to reef down. The main has roller reefing, while the mizzen and the jib have reef points.

Accommodation is divided between three cabins in a fairly standard layout. The forward and after cabins each have two berths and the settee in the main saloon converts into a double. The galley on the port side is adjacent to the accommodation access. Clear plastic locker fronts enable the contents to be seen and give a more spacious appearance to the cabin.

Deck layout is practical and obviously has been given a great deal of thought. However, the anchor stowed in the pipe could be liable to jam after pounding into a head sea. A good non-slip covering is on all of the deck, not just the areas most in use as is often the case. The coachroof tops are teak planked, which reduces the 'plastic' appearance associated with fibreglass. Guardrails are stainless steel tubing all round, in place of the more normal wire and stanchions. The tubing provides a more substantial safety barrier, but is much more liable to bending when alongside a quay or another boat. Access to the after cabin is from the cockpit, which means it faces forward; however it is fairly well protected by the extended roof of the shelter and the high cockpit sides.

The Coaster demonstrates how closely the requirements of both sail and power can be met in one hull. The sailing performance is very adequate and I am sure that in time a larger engine will be fitted to fully realize the motoring potential.

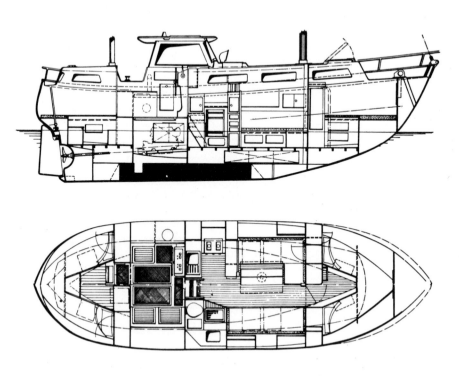

LOA	32′ 9″	10 m	Sail areas:	main	220 ft^2	20.5 m^2
LWL	28′ 5″	8.7 m		jib	236 ft^2	22 m^2
Beam	10′ 2″	3.1 m		mizzen	70 ft^2	6.5 m^2
Draft	4′	1.2 m	Engine	BMC Captain diesel		
Displ	18,000 lb	8,000 kg	Fuel	75 Imp gal/90 US gal/340 litres		
Ballast	6,400 lb	2,900 kg	Water	80 Imp gal/96 US gal/360 litres		

Built by R J Prior & Son Ltd, Burnham-on-Crouch, Essex, UK; designed by Alan F Hill.

Endurance 40

Ferrocement is now used worldwide for yachts, working boats, barges and fishing boats, but the Endurance 40 is unique in being a production motorsailer built in this material. The hull thickness averages about 1 in, and apart from shallow stiffening frames and floor and engine bearers, the interior is clean. Bulkheads are fitted to divide the interior space and support joinery rather than to stiffen the hull.

The shape of the hull is a good compromise between power and sailing requirements. Transverse sections are full amidships; the profile from the deck to the top of the keel has a very pronounced curve and the turn at the bilge is fairly sharp, giving good stability and allowing plenty of room inside. The stability thus produced by the shape has to compensate for the relatively low ballast ratio: 6,500 lb (3,000 kg) on a displacement of 41,400 lb (18,800 kg). While extra weight in the form of ballast is not being carried, on the other hand a full shape requires more power to drive it through the water than a finer one.

The transom is large for this type of boat, and does expose a large flat surface to the wind and waves in a following sea. As the transom is well clear of the water this should not pose any particular problem as the stern should lift before seas hit it. At the bow, the full sections amidships run into a slight flare intended to deflect water and spray; it is kept slight to balance the full sections at the stern. In profile the bow is unusual in being what is termed a 'clipper' bow, to give a pleasing line to the hull where it terminates in the bowsprit. The clipper bow emphasizes the forefoot, which is compensated for by the sharply reversed line into the straight keel.

The keel is fairly long, which should make for directional stability while the sharp upturns at each end still allow easy turning. It is also very wide (as is often the case with ferro hulls) and although well tapered at each end must interfere with the water flow past the propeller and reduce its efficiency. The propeller is set fairly high, no doubt to enable the shaft line to be as nearly horizontal as possible, but if the shaft had been lower or angled more the propeller would have been working in cleaner water. The rudder shape is unusual but effective with most of the area concentrated at the bottom of the blade. It is balanced, but only slightly, and the large area could make the steering heavy. With a lower propeller, steering under power would have been more effective because of the larger area of rudder which the propeller thrust could act against.

A four-cylinder Perkins 4-236 diesel engine (72 h.p. intermittent one-hour rating at 2,500 r.p.m.) is installed under the wheelhouse with conventional drive to a three-bladed 20 in (0.5 m) propeller. For the heavy displacement this is only just adequate power, and the Endurance 40 is very much sailing oriented. Alternative engines of lower horsepower (e.g. Perkins 4-154) can be installed. Fuel and water tankage are also variable.

Although the overall form has some interesting features, the basic shape is fairly traditional. This is a realistic approach when building a non-racing boat in a new material. Although the hull is made from ferrocement, the remainder is fairly orthodox. The teak deck is laid over plywood on wooden shelves and beams, and

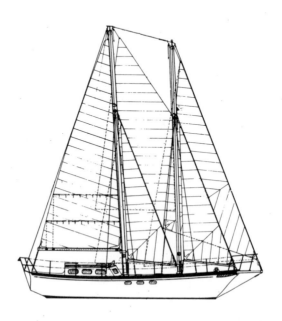

is flush except for the cockpit and wheelhouse. The overall size of the boat allows plenty of headroom even with the flush deck. The low wheelhouse, which in profile is more like a long doghouse, enhances the sleek lines, but visibility ahead is very restricted. The helmsman's eye level is only just above the deck, and the sheer means that he will be blind for several points on each bow; heeling could also interfere with the sideways visibility. The outside steering position is much better in this respect. The wheelhouse is large and also serves as a saloon and navigating area (and in one version, contains the galley). While all the crew can be together in this area during the day without overcrowding, there could be conflicting demands on the use of the space. The engine compartment hatches are in the sole.

The standard rig is a ketch, but a schooner version is offered as an alternative. In both, a bowsprit allows two headsails to be set and helps to keep sail areas down to manageable sizes. The basic ketch has about 940 sq ft (90 m^2) of working sail area; on the schooner this is increased to around 1,200 sq ft (110 m^2) by completely filling in the area between the two masts, but with the drawback of heavier masts and perhaps a somewhat reduced closehauled performance.

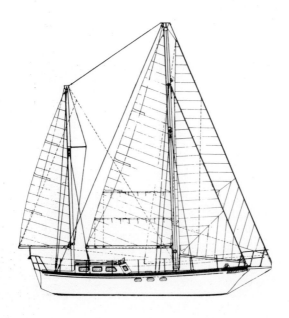

The accommodation layout can be varied to suit individual requirements, but the basic designs divide it into four or three separate cabins in addition to shared spaces. Although this solution gives privacy, it does create small cabins and a 'congested' appearance down below. The forepeak contains a pipecot and workbench, useful for long passages and cruising generally.

The Endurance 40 has been designed and built as a long-range cruising boat in the true motorsailer sense. The strong hull, low superstructure and small cockpit should enable it to tackle rough conditions without difficulty. The relatively low cost of the ferro-cement hull enables the builders to offer an individual and flexible approach to finishing to owners' preferences and yet maintain a competitive price.

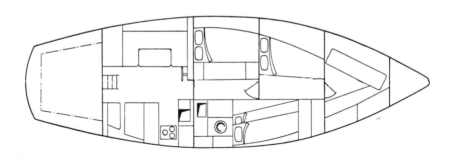

LOA	48' 6"	14.8 m			
Hull	41' 6"	12.7 m	Working sails:	ketch	760 ft² 80 m²
LWL	31' 2"	9.5 m		schooner	1,200 ft² 110 m²
Beam	12' 5"	3.8 m	Engine	Perkins 4-236 diesel	
Draft	5' 9"	1.8 m	Fuel	100 Imp gal/120 US gal/450 litres	
Displ	51,400 lb	18,800 kg	Water	150 Imp gal/180 US gal/680 litres	
Ballast	6,500 lb	3,000 kg			

Built by Windboats Ltd, Wroxham, Norfolk, U K; designed by Peter Ibold.

Euros 41

A great deal of thought has been put into this French motorsailer in order to produce good performance under both sail and motor. While the accent is on sailing, with a speed of 9 knots under power it can hardly be said that the other aspect has been neglected. The hull has nearly pure sailing lines, with what almost amounts to a fin keel with the ballast placed at its extremity. The boat is very light for its size and the ballast ratio is high: this is necessary to compensate for the lack of stability derived from hull form. The beam is narrow for the length, but the sharp turn of the bilge partly compensates for this. The relatively light weight and somewhat angular configuration would make this hull lively in a seaway, but this is part of the price which has to be paid for performance. The sections are moderately full at bow and stern and there is a long run of the counter up to the transom stern. At speeds over 7 knots the stern would be sucked down, effectively increasing the waterline length allowing a higher speed, but at the same time increasing the skin friction so that considerable extra power will be needed to achieve the maximum of 9 knots. At slow speeds this part of the hull is above water, lowering the total resistance. Cruising speed is given as 8.3 knots.

The short keel should make the boat very responsive to the helm, and the skeg forward of the rudder also aids manoeuvrability. It supports the rudder bearings and gives a degree of protection from floating objects, and by being separate from the keel the rudder can be placed well aft where it is most effective.

Fitting the three-bladed propeller into a tight aperture in the skeg does not give a good flow of water for the propeller to work in. The clearances between the propeller and the edges of the aperture are small, further reducing efficiency. On the other hand the propeller is close to the rudder, so that steering under power will be improved even though the rudder is not balanced. If the propeller had been placed just aft of the keel it could have worked more effectively in terms of propulsion, but with a normal drive

the engine casing would then have intruded on the accommodation. A V-drive with the engine in its present position but turned end-for-end would have given a better position for the propeller, but adds complication, cost and weight.

There is very little sheer to the deck line, which does not reduce the space below amidships. Further headroom is gained from the unusual stepped coachroof; this also helps to reduce its bulk and improves the overall appearance of the boat. The coachroof is kept sensibly narrow in order to leave wide side decks for easy and safe movement. The cockpit is of a reasonable size, but the protection offered by the shelter is fairly minimal. Any spray coming on board from the side, where most of it seems to originate, would have free access to the cockpit, the only person getting much protection being the helmsman. The layout clearly demonstrates the main disadvantage of after cabins, namely their exposed access; here access is via the cockpit, and the space beneath the cockpit sole is taken up by the engine and large lockers. The engine access hatches in the cockpit sole are watertight, and the cockpit is self-draining as is the ingenious anchor stowage forward. It keeps the anchor well out of the way, yet ready for immediate use if required, and uses space which would otherwise be wasted.

The present engine is a four-cylinder Volvo Penta diesel (max. rating 75 h.p.) mounted at a fairly steep angle because of the short distance between it and the propeller. Bilge and waste pumps run off the engine; the net shaft h.p. at cruising speed is 50 h.p. In the compact installation the fuel tanks are mounted on each side of the engine compartment. The contents can be checked visually by means of clear plastic gauges on the after saloon bulkhead. The engine compartment also contains the air and water heaters, which are both heat exchangers working off the engine cooling system. The (cold) water tank is moulded into the keel above the ballast, thus utilizing what would otherwise be wasted space, but with the disadvantage that using up water could have a considerable effect on the height of the centre of gravity and thus the stability. The tank filler pipe forms one of the supports for the cabin table and a handhold in the cabin.

Much ingenuity has been shown in designing the accommodation and full use has been made of all the available space. A maximum of eight people can sleep aboard; two of the berths are double. Full use of all these berths would make the boat very crowded, and a more realistic number would be five. The galley is at the after end of the main saloon with a good-sized chart table opposite. Unusually for this size of boat, there are two toilets, one forward and one in the after cabin.

As befits a motorsailer with such an emphasis on sailing, the wardrobe is comprehensive. The standard set includes two jibs and two genoas, main and mizzen; the only optional sail is a spinnaker. The tall, light aluminium mast gives the mainsail a high aspect ratio, and a similar shape is in the mizzen. Unusually, the mainsail is not fitted with roller reefing, three sets of reef points being used instead. Reefing would perhaps not be required as frequently on a ketch rigged boat. The mizzen has two rows of reef points.

The Euros 41 represents a great deal of modern thinking in a sailing-oriented type of motorsailer. Though it might be called a full-powered auxiliary as opposed to a motorsailer, the sheltered steering position brings it within the motorsailer category. Certainly its balanced performance is very much that of a motorsailer, with a maximum of 9 knots available under both power and sail.

			Sail areas:			
LOA	40' 6"	12.35 m		main	260 ft^2	24 m^2
LWL	31' 10"	9.7 m		jib	200 ft^2	19 m^2
Beam	10' 10"	3.3 m		mizzen	120 ft^2	11 m^2
Draft	5' 5"	1.7 m		genoas	330 ft^2	31 m^2
Displ	15,000 lb	7,000 kg			480 ft^2	45 m^2
Ballast	5,500 lb	2,500 kg	Fuel	55 Imp gal/66 US gal/250 litres		
Engine	75 h.p. Volvo Penta diesel		Water	104 Imp gal/124 US gal/470 litres		

Built by Chantiers Amel in La Rochelle-Périgny, France; designed by H Amel.

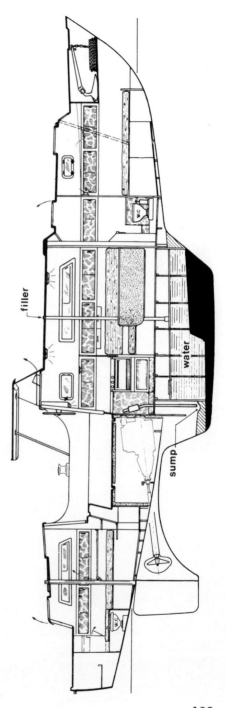

Finnsailer 35

Over six hundred of this class have been built in Finland by Turku Boatyard. The hull is taken directly from a North Sea pilot boat and has very pleasing lines; while clearly motor-oriented, sailing performance is very good. The curves and shapes are smooth and cohesive and it looks seaworthy. A slight incongruity is found in the bow where its flare and the reversed line of the stem do not quite match the full cruiser stern. However, the flare is practical and keeps down spray, particularly when sailing heeled.

The keel runs in a smooth line from the bow with a moderate forefoot. The ballast keel is an added section below the keel proper and runs for perhaps two-thirds of the overall length from aft; it serves the double function of protecting the fibreglass and deepening the after part of the hull to improve steering. Transverse sections are full amidships to give good form stability. Unusually for a motorsailer, there are twin bilge keels amidships which run for about a quarter of the length and reduce rolling. (A full hull such as this with little in the way of a keel projection offers less resistance to rolling.) They are not deep enough to keep it upright when sitting on the bottom. The stern has a pleasing shape very reminiscent of fishing vessels, and should contribute to behaving well in a following sea (2.3). The full amidships sections taper into the deadwood at the after end of which is the propeller aperture. This gives a good flow of water to the large three-bladed propeller. The rudder lies behind the propeller, with the lower rudder bearing carried on a skeg which extends under the propeller; it has a slight degree of balancing.

Steering under power is excellent and gives precise control. The long keel gives good directional stability, but also makes the boat sluggish to turn when tacking under sail. In a strong wind it will come round if moving rapidly, but in light winds there is insufficient momentum and a short burst on the engine may be necessary.

Two steering wheels are fitted to a hydraulic steering system and can be used independently without disconnecting. The inner steering position is in the shelter and has the engine controls and gauges to hand. The helmsman has a comfortable seat and a hatch is provided in the shelter roof so that he can stand and get a good view when manoeuvring. The outer wheel is on a pedestal in the cockpit, from which there is a good view of the sails. Both are well placed, the only discordant note being the small wheels with projecting spokes.

The pleasing lines of the hull are rather spoiled by a large, high coachroof which is meant to give plenty of space below and is taken right aft to form the cockpit coaming. Large windows in the coachroof sides give plenty of light below, but they are vulnerable to waves. Its bulk is emphasized by the steering shelter being in the same material and colour: a great deal could have been done to improve the appearance by the subtle use of contrasting colours or materials. However, the deck line has a very pleasant sheer delineated by a contrasting rubbing strip.

The layout of the accommodation and cockpit have been carefully thought out and the space used sensibly. The temptation to squeeze in as many berths as possible has been resisted, and this 35 ft (11 m) hull has four comfortable berths which can be used without any modification. A fifth can be made available by converting one berth into a double berth. The space in the main cabin looks restricted because the full width of the boat is not visible, but otherwise the interior is spacious and well fitted out. The galley adjacent to the wheelhouse companionway is particularly well planned for use at sea. An electric extractor fan draws air from both the bilges and the galley area to give good circulation.

The large cockpit suits a cruising boat and gives plenty of space to move about. The Perkins 4-236 diesel engine (72 h.p. intermittent one-hour rating at 2,500 r.p.m.) is mounted under the cockpit floor between the two shelter seats, but the lockers on each side of the cockpit make access a little difficult. Soundproofing of the engine compartment is very good. Two 50 Imp gal (60 US gal or 230 litres) fuel tanks on either side of the engine give a range under power of about 600 miles.

A great deal of space is available for equipment stowage, essential for all the miscellaneous gear found to be necessary on a cruising boat. There is even a special locker for bonded stores.

A foredeck hatch gives access to an anchor stowage space in the forepeak.

The simple sail plan is contained well within the length of the boat. In fact the forestay meets the deck just forward of the coachroof, leaving the space in the bows clear for handling the anchor and warps. The jib is almost as large as the mainsail, which makes for good performance but means that it has to be helped from side to side when tacking. A genoa and spinnaker are obtainable as optional extras and would greatly improve light wind performance.

The Finnsailer 35 is a very practical motorsailer, well constructed and finished. It performs well under motor, and will sail well with the wind abeam or aft. Closehauled performance is not so good, the shallow draft allowing the hull to make excessive leeway; to make worthwhile progress to windward would need the assistance of the engine. While overall appearance leaves something to be desired, it is a change to find practical considerations taking priority.

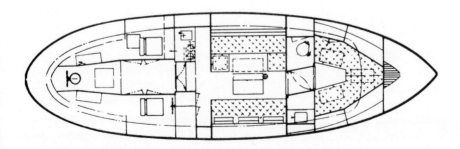

LOA	34' 9"	10.6 m	Sail areas:	main	198 ft²	18.4 m²
LWL	30' 8"	9.4 m		jib	174 ft²	16.2 m²
Beam	10' 3"	3.1 m		reacher	229 ft²	21.3 m²
Draft	4' 4"	1.3 m	Engine	Perkins 4-236M diesel		
Displ	15,400 lb	7,000 kg	Fuel	92 Imp gal/110 US gal/420 litres		
Ballast	3,700 lb	1,700 kg	Water	60 Imp gal/72 US gal/270 litres		

Built and designed by Oy Fiskars AB, Turun Veneviestämö (Turku Boatyard), Turku, Finland.

Fjord MS33

Many of the desirable features only found on large motorsailers are fitted here into a hull only 33 ft (10 m) long. Not only is the hull of a moderate size, but the designer has not had to resort to a transom stern to gain more space, and the boat is very attractive to look at, showing its origins in its typical Scandinavian double-ended shape and definite sheer of the deck line.

Study of the hull shape reveals very pleasing lines. The full shape of the stern is nicely balanced by a slight flare at the bow; it is not very conspicuous as it terminates in a slight knuckle which runs into the rubbing strip, extending the knuckle line right aft. The maximum beam is aft of amidships and large in relation to the length. This gives good stability characteristics without having to resort to a lot of ballast, although the ballast ratio is still high; it has been largely influenced by the large sail area and moderately light displacement.

Under water, the keel is long and very wide for the size of hull. The width of the bottom of the keel amidships is 12 in (0.3 m), which enables the boat to rest on its own keel, although of course it wouldn't balance when taking the bottom in harbour without additional support. The keel is well faired to give a good flow of water to the propeller, but the interruption is emphasized by the two-bladed propeller, giving considerable vibration as the blades are alternately blanked and uncovered by the deadwood. The interesting rudder shape is partly balanced and gives very good and responsive steering. Only the lower half of the rudder produces the balancing effect, so that the thrust from the propeller is not fully utilized in steering. Having the lower bearing of the rudder only half-way down the blade puts a higher strain on the bearings, and leaves a large part of the rudder unsupported. It also means that the rudder and shaft are not shielded from damage by the skeg, so the rudder cannot take any weight. The long keel provides some protection.

The full shape amidships is carried well down on the hull, and apart from giving form stability allows the engine to be sited low down. This further helps stability by lowering the centre of gravity, and gives a nearly horizontal shaft line, making the propeller more efficient. Keeping the engine low means that the top of the wheelhouse can also be kept low, which gives a sleeker overall appearance. The low bulwarks augment the effect by making the forward coachroof less apparent. An interesting feature of the fibreglass hull moulding is simulated planking seams. While they help to reduce any 'clinical' look, they must catch dirt and make cleaning the hull more difficult. The light horizontal seam lines do help to reduce the apparent freeboard, and the contrasting colour of the rubbing strake also helps.

The mast is high in comparison with the overall length and nearly amidships. This gives the mainsail a high aspect ratio which makes for more efficiency and also keeps its size down to manageable proportions. The standard sails are simply a No. 1 jib and a main, but no less than ten additional sails are offered as extras. Fairly unique among motorsailers is the use of a spinnaker. Great attention has been paid to sailing performance.

The engine (under the wheelhouse floor) is a four-cylinder Perkins 4-108 diesel giving up to 49 h.p. at 4,000 r.p.m. (intermittent one-hour rating), fairly low power for a motorsailer of this size, although the low hull weight compensates to some extent. The two-bladed propeller does not transmit power as effectively as a three-bladed one, and the performance under power is only just adequate for a motorsailer. A propeller shaft brake is a standard fitting; a spring-loaded device engages a pin on the shaft, locking the propeller in the vertical position behind the deadwood.

The main steering position is in the cockpit, for sailing. Steering is hydraulic and either wheel can be used at any time without any disconnecting being necessary. The secondary position is in the wheelhouse, and it is here that the engine instruments are sited, and an alarm buzzer for oil pressure and temperature. The navigation table is by the wheelhouse steering position and also forms the helmsman's seat, which might cause some conflict.

The wheelhouse and main saloon are separated by a half bulkhead to give spaciousness. With the accommodation area open right through, the wheelhouse doors have to be able to keep the sea out. They are on the large side and almost on a level with the

cockpit sole, and a sea taken there could quickly find its way below. Some modifications would be required for serious cruising, and it is to the builders' credit that they recognize this and make recommendations for boards to be placed in the opening. A good feature is the manual which is supplied to each owner; it should enable him to find his way round and get the best out of his boat.

The accommodation is well fitted out, with five berths. Two are in the form of a dinette which converts to a double berth; one is in the wheelhouse, which at sea would only be suitable for a heavy sleeper or a conscientious skipper. The galley is comprehensively equipped, with a refrigerator, stove and plenty of stowage space. In common with most Scandinavian motorsailers, the stove is of the alcohol type.

A great deal of original thought has gone into the Fjord MS33's design, and the result is generally very pleasing in terms of both practicality and appearance.

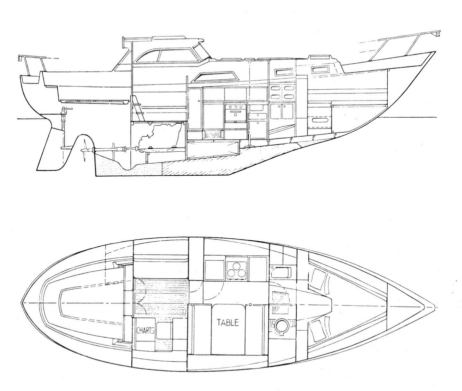

LOA	32′ 11″	10.0 m	Sail areas:	main	200 ft^2	18.5 m^2
LWL	26′ 3″	8.0 m		jib	260 ft^2	24.5 m^2
Beam	10′ 6″	3.2 m		genoas	300 ft^2	28 m^2
Draft	4′ 5″	1.4 m			350 ft^2	32.5 m^2
Displ	15,400 lb	7,000 kg	Fuel	44 Imp gal/53 US gal/200 litres		
Ballast	5,500 lb	2,500 kg	Water	Same		
Engine	Perkins 4-108 diesel					

Built by A/S Fjord Plast, Arendal, Norway; designed by Eivind Amble.

Lohi/Joemarin 34

The Lohi 34 (previously known as the Joemarin 34) is a Finnish motorsailer with the accent very much on sailing. She looks every inch a sailing boat and incorporates a lot of the latest thinking, yet she performs well under motor and the accommodation matches up to the best motorsailers. Much original thinking has gone into this design, and it demonstrates how the modern sailing-oriented motorsailer could be better described as a fully powered sailing auxiliary.

The hull is clearly derived from racing yachts, though beamier for greater stability and accommodation space. The beam is carried well down to full bilges which taper into the keel. The draft is relatively deep for a motorsailer of this size but in keeping with the sailing emphasis, and must contribute to the good windward performance. The forefoot is sharp and then runs gently into the keel. The after edge of the fin keel is cut off sharp apart from its top section which runs aft in a sort of 'bustle' to contain and support the propeller shaft; the rudder is on a separate skeg aft of the propeller. This profile is a moderate version of that on many modern sailing yachts.

The present engine is a 36 h.p. Volvo Penta MD3 diesel, which is low power for this size of motorsailer (a 47 h.p. engine was originally fitted). While adequate for moderate seas, it could be a little lacking in power under really adverse conditions. The drive to the propeller is conventional, but the two-bladed propeller is consistent with the sailing emphasis.

The sheerline is almost straight, but its slight curvature is complemented by the reverse sheer of the superstructure. By carrying the superstructure to the full width of the boat and fitting small windows in the sides, a great deal of space has been created down below. Hull and superstructure are in contrasting colours, which avoids a bulky look and gives very sleek lines. The dark rubbing strip emphasizes this line, and the boat is a good example of how carefully chosen contrasting colours can be used

to improve overall appearance.

The optional wheel shelter is low, to maintain the sleek profile, and joins a very low coachroof. The shelter gives very little protection to the helmsman, and in fact does little more than protect the access to the main accommodation and any navigation instruments. It can be extended aft by means of a folding canvas canopy but this is unlikely to be used much at sea.

As would be expected, a very complete set of sails is supplied as standard. The sail plan has a high aspect ratio, and performance is very good in both light and strong winds – it can hold its own with most sailing yachts of similar size. The only optional sail is a spinnaker, and no less than four alternative headsails are supplied, with roller reefing on the main.

While the Joemarin 34 shows many advanced features outside, it is in the interior layout that the motorsailer concept of comfort and practicality really shows. Provision is made for six comfortable berths while still retaining a separate settee and table,

so that no alterations have to be made for different living functions. The fore cabin berths are staggered so that each is full size; this leaves space to starboard for the toilet/shower compartment. In the saloon two berths are on the starboard side one above the other, but offset to follow the shape of the hull. The upper is fitted with a deep leeboard and curtains and looks a very snug place to sleep at sea. The lower berth serves also as a settee, but is supplementary to the main L-shaped settee which fits around the table on the port side. The full width of the hull has been exploited and gives a good effect of space.

The galley, just aft of the settee on the port side, is comprehensively equipped with stove, refrigerator, sink and self-draining crockery locker. Across from the galley on the starboard side is the chart table, which is very large for a boat of this size. The only criticism here is that it faces aft, which can disorient the navigator and lead to mistakes. The remaining two berths are in an after cabin, reached from a small stern cockpit which offers some protection to the access but does mean clambering out on deck. It is a little cramped, but adequate for sleeping.

A paraffin (kerosene) heater mounted right in the stern pumps warm air to all three compartments ensuring not only warmth but a good circulation through the boat. In warm weather a separate ventilation system ducts fresh air to outlets low down in

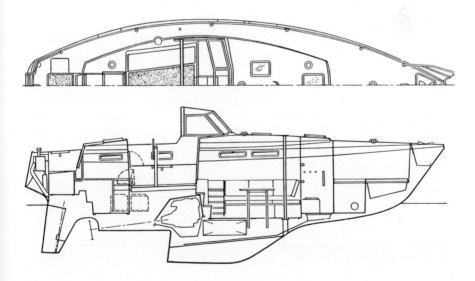

each compartment. Stale air is expelled through ventilators in the cabin tops, and the whole system ensures good circulation under all conditions, but electric fans are used which do drain the battery.

The internal decor has received a great deal of care and uses interesting materials and colours not normally found on boats. The result is a very pleasant and warm atmosphere, which combined with the apparent spaciousness makes living on board very comfortable. With its exceptional sailing qualities, the Joemarin 34 is a very viable modern motorsailer.

LOA	34′ 1″	10.4 m	Sail areas:	main	237 ft²	22 m²
LWL	28′ 6″	8.7 m		jib	220 ft²	20.5 m²
Beam	10′ 4″	3.2 m		storm jib	140 ft²	13 m²
Draft	4′ 9″	1.5 m		genoa	377 ft²	35 m²
Displ	12,100 lb	5,500 kg		lt gen	452 ft²	42 m²
Ballast	4,850 lb	2,200 kg	Fuel	40 Imp gal/48 US gal/180 litres		
Engine	Volvo Penta MD3 diesel		Water	50 Imp gal/60 US gal/230 litres		

Built by Lohi Oy (previously known as Joemarin Oy), Joensuu, Finland; designed by Hans Groop.

Pelagian

In an interesting attempt to produce a hull which fully meets the motorsailer requirement the Pelagian has achieved performance under power in excess of that of which a pure displacement hull of this size is capable. Its twin engines are unique among small motorsailers.

The hull was developed with the aid of tank tests and conforms closely to the semi-displacement type. The full shape forward and amidships tapers off into a long flat run aft. At full speed the bow lifts and the stern squats; the flat run aft attains a certain amount of lift from the forward motion of the boat, thus reducing total wetted surface and hence friction. The lift also reduces the wave-making resistance, allowing the top speed to exceed that predicted for the displacement mode.

The development of this design illustrates some of the practical problems involved. Tank testing indicated that the hull would theoretically be capable of 12 knots maximum speed. To attain this meant that the displacement (the total weight of the boat, rig, fuel, engines etc) had to be kept within the design specification while sufficient power had to be available to propel it up to this speed. Twin 2.5 L four-cylinder BMC Commander diesels (50 h.p. at 3,000 r.p.m.) were found to provide ample power for this purpose, but their weight required compensating lightening of the boat's construction. The builders found that twin BMC 1.5 L Captain diesels (32 b.h.p. at 3,000 r.p.m.) would push the boat at 10 knots maximum, were 500 lb lighter (allowing the heavier hull construction desired by the builders), and could be installed far more accessibly in the space available. This solution, though a slight compromise on the original intention, is more satisfactory to the builders and is likely to be so for the owners, in terms of trouble-free longevity of hull and engines.

The ballast ratio is low, as one would expect. The full sections amidships and generous beam help to compensate, and the weight of the centreplate when lowered also aids stability. The design

of the centreplate is interesting in that it does not intrude on the cabin: the pivoted plate retracts into the keel and the operating lever enters the boat between the engines. A hand-operated hydraulic ram forces the plate down when required, thus reducing the chances of it jamming, but there remains the risk of a fault in the hydraulics.

The ballast and engines are placed fairly well aft so that the bow can lift and the flat sections aft can then come into full effect to give the whole hull lift. In section the hull has full bilges which run into a flat section at the centre of the hull. Instead of the bottom tapering into the keel, here the keel is almost in the form of a fin so that the bottom is as flat as possible. The hull tapers in from amidships to the stern and terminates in a forward-sloping transom (3.4). This carries the flat bottom surfaces right aft and gives maximum lift, preventing the stern from squatting excessively.

The single rudder is mounted right aft for maximum effect, supported by a separate skeg (6.3). It is not balanced and obtains only minimal effect from the propeller thrust. This is compensated for by its position right aft and gives a good compromise in view of the wide speed range of this boat. The propellers are on each side of the hull just forward of the rudder skeg. To get the necessary clearance between the hull and the propellers, the shafts are exposed for several feet from where they leave the hull just below the turn of the bilge. The end of each shaft is supported in an A-bracket, and these brackets, the propellers and the shafts cause considerable drag when sailing (6.3).

The performance under sail cannot compare with that under power, although the sail area carried is large in relation to the displacement. The mast height is nearly equal to the overall length, but the displacement is low for the length of hull. The mizzen boom extends beyond the transom and the jib is larger in area than the mainsail. This might disturb the sail balance when under reduced sail particularly as the main underwater areas of the hull are aft. The centreplate is also aft of the centre point and may also upset the balance.

The deck line has only a slight sheer, and as when under way at full speed the bow lifts and the stern squats, the deck then slopes aft for the whole of its length. This bow-up attitude does not enhance the appearance, and the raised bow reduces visibility forward. Deck space is obstructed to the extent that moving about is not easy; the side decks are narrow and are further obstructed by the sheet winch bases and engine air intakes (3.4). Plenty of handholds are provided to make movement safe even though a little difficult.

The flatness of the hull reduces the internal headroom and a moderately high coachroof has had to be employed. On this length of hull the high coachroof gives a somewhat stunted appearance to the boat and its abrupt forward termination accentuates this. The angular shelter at the steering position does not give a pleasant flowing line, and the whole effect is somewhat fussy.

The shelter also offers very little protection for the helmsman. The wheel is situated at the after end of the cockpit to allow a good view of the sails, and as there are no side screens in the shelter crew in the cockpit have little protection from spray. It is difficult to see any valid purpose for the shelter except to protect the entrance to the forward accommodation.

Within the confines of this smallish hull, the accommodation has been carefully laid out. There is little room for luxuries, but the basic necessities are there. Both the after and forward cabins

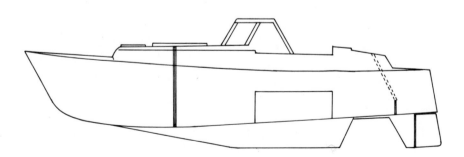

have two berths but little room for anything else. An interesting feature in the after cabin is the sloping support for the mizzen mast, so contrived so that it doesn't intrude more than necessary. The bulkhead at the forward end of the saloon provides support for the mainmast which is stepped on deck.

The Pelagian represents a bold attempt to get better performance from a motorsailer, particularly under power. In gaining this extra performance, which is a considerable increase over what could normally be expected, several features have suffered, notably appearance and accommodation. Clever design has minimized the impact on the latter and no doubt development will improve the appearance. It is possible that the designer erred in choosing a small size of motorsailer in which to attempt to get extra speed: the task might have been easier and the compromises less exacting if a larger hull had been used as the basis of the design. However, the Pelagian certainly offers several features which no other motorsailer offers and could point the way to future developments. It is original thinking such as this which leads eventually to the production of better and more efficient boats.

LOA	33′	10.1 m	Sail areas:	main	170 ft^2	16 m^2
LWL	30′ 3″	9.2 m		jib	190 ft^2	17 m^2
Beam	9′ 6″	2.9 m		mizzen	67 ft^2	6 m^2
Draft	3′ 6″	1.1 m (keel up)		genoa	295 ft^2	27 m^2
	5′ 9″	1.8 m (keel down)	Engines	Twin BMC Captain diesels		
Displ	11,250 lb	5,000 kg	Fuel	80 Imp gal/96 US gal/360 litres		
Ballast	2,800 lb	1,270 kg (fixed)	Water	40 Imp gal/48 US gal/180 litres		
	1,300 lb	590 kg (engines + drop keel)				

Built by Macwester Marine Co. Ltd, Littlehampton, Sussex, UK; designed by C S J Roy.

Southerly 28

A very original approach to both hull shape and fitting out, the Southerly 28 is small compared to many motorsailers, but this probably represents the builders' caution in trying out a new concept. Now that this design is proving itself, there is every encouragement to experiment with a larger version.

The aim was to produce a boat which would have good performance under both motor and sail, and at the same time be capable of taking the bottom, thus opening up a much wider market as so many moorings dry out on each tide. It was logical to have a centreboard, so that reduced fixed draft could be combined with good windward performance. If the centreboard was not to intrude on the cabin space it had to be recessed into the stub keel, which houses the ballast as well. The ballast keel projects about a foot below the hull, and if the boat is to sit reasonably upright some form of side support is needed. Bilge keels provide this, but their function is not as simple as on most twin-keelers. They are asymmetrical in section and extend about a foot from the hull, placed just below the turn of the bilge on the flatter part of the bottom so that they are nearly vertical, and are toed in slightly at the after ends. This tends to trap the water flowing past between the bilge keels and the keel proper, and imparts lift to the hull, enhanced by the flat run aft up to the transom. The Southerly will run at about 10 knots with the 25 h.p. Volvo Penta M D2B diesel engine fitted, a speed in excess of that of which a purely displacement hull of this size would be capable, which shows that it is obtaining lift. However, the hull is fibreglass and the surfaces which come in contact with the bottom can be expected to show wear and even damage, especially at their edges.

Light displacement must go a long way to giving this sort of performance. The ballast ratio is high, balancing a good area of sail so that up to 9 knots can be expected. The normal rig using the standard genoa is 324 sq ft (30 m²) which for a boat of this

size gives very good performance. The mast is almost amidships for balance as the bilge keels extend the underwater area well aft.

Above the waterline the bow flares outward and the full sections are carried aft, with a gentle knuckle just above the waterline to deflect spray and increase space inside. To reduce the bulkiness of the hull, the lower (hull) moulding terminates a few inches below the deck level and the sides are continued upwards as part of the deck moulding; they taper in slightly and the effect is to give a full-width coachroof running aft to the cockpit and joining the cockpit coaming. With this type of construction great care has to be taken with the join between the hull and deck mouldings as it is in a vulnerable position; here it is covered with a moulded PVC extrusion.

The coachroof proper is kept low and slopes upwards to the wheelhouse. The boat looks nicely proportioned, the only incongruous note being the returned line at the upper part of the bow. Large, sharp-cornered windows in each side of the hull look a little vulnerable, and could well be under water when the boat is heeled to a stiff breeze. On deck, a self-draining well forward is for the anchor or warps. The cockpit is spacious and has large lockers which can hold most of the spare gear which every boat seems to collect.

The rudder is hung outboard of the large transom and a small skeg behind the propeller aperture supports its lower bearing. This is a practical if slightly inefficient arrangement, and at least gives the crew a chance to do something if the rudder jams. It is commendable to find two steering positions on a boat of this size: the outside position in the cockpit is obtained by the simple expedient of fitting a tiller to the rudderhead; the other is in the wheelhouse.

Maximum use has been made of the interior space, with five berths one of which is a quarter berth under the wheelhouse steering position. However, it is unlikely to be tenable at sea. The dinette in the main saloon converts into a double berth, with support for its after edge provided by the centreboard case. Forward there are two full-size berths at different heights, to overcome the usual disadvantages of V-berths. The whole of the starboard side of the saloon is taken up by the galley, giving the cook plenty of space. This area is divided from the inner steering position by a half bulkhead, but not totally cut off. At first glance the toilet compartment looks badly placed, taking up about a third of the wheelhouse. However, there is a certain logic in putting it there, where it can be used when at sea without disturbing those sleeping below or leaving the deck. It also has full headroom, rather than requiring the contortions often associated with using

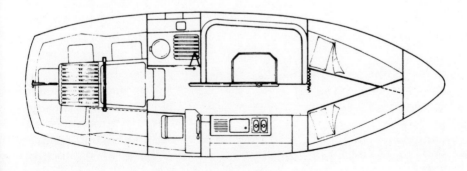

the heads at sea. Visibility from the steering position is maintained by having a window in the door of the toilet compartment.

The Southerly 28 is a bold experiment to advance the potential of the motorsailer. It has succeeded in terms of speed, but speed is not everything and only time will prove the acceptability of this novel design. However, the logic of the approach should give it a good start.

			Sail areas:			
LOA	27' 6"	8.4 m		main	149 ft^2	14 m^2
LWL	24'	7.3 m		jib	98 ft^2	9 m^2
Beam	9'	2.7 m		genoa	175 ft^2	16 m^2
Draft	2' 6"	.8 m (board up)		lt gen	250 ft^2	23 m^2
	4' 9"	1.5 m (board down)	Engine	Volvo Penta MD2B diesel		
Displ	8,500 lb	3,860 kg	Fuel	25 Imp gal/30 US gal/110 litres		
Ballast	2,900 lb	1,300 kg (fixed)	Water	35 Imp gal/42 US gal/160 litres		

Built by Northshore Yacht Yards Ltd, Itchenor Shipyard, Itchenor, Chichester, Sussex, UK; designed by John A Bennett.